CITY OF PHILADELPHIA

Proclamation

Whereas...

Over the years, Philadelphia's wealth of fine arts and its programs for the encouragement of art and architecture have made it a model for similar efforts throughout the nation; and

WHEREAS...

Time has confirmed the vision of the landmark ordinance of 1959 which required that fine arts be included in all public establishments and that art should be placed where the public can enjoy it; and

WHEREAS...

This Fine Arts Program has stimulated city planners, architects and artists to provide public art of the highest quality; and

WHEREAS...

During the period March 19 through April 30, 1980 the Institute of Contemporary Art at the University of Pennsylvania will focus on Philadelphia's public art in a multi-media show, and will publish a map locating the sculpture derived through the Fine Arts Ordinance:

Now, Therefore...

I, William J. Green, Mayor of the City of Philadelphia, do hereby proclaim Tuesday, March 18, 1980 as

PUBLIC ART DAY

in this city, do salute the new exhibition of the Institute of Contemporary Art, and do urge all the citizens to enjoy Philadelphia's art and this show to the fullest.

William J. Green

MAYOR

Given under my hand and the Seal of the City of Philadelphia, this eighteenth day of March, one thousand, nine hundred and eighty.

CITY OF PHILADELPHIA

Proclamation

Whereas ...

Over the years, Philadelphia's wealth of fine arts and its programs for the encouragement of art and architecture have made it a model for similar efforts throughout the nation; and

WHEREAS ...

Time has confirmed the vision of the landmark ordinance of 1959 which required that fine arts be included in all public establishments and that art should be placed where the public can enjoy it; and

WHEREAS ...

This Fine Arts Program has stimulated city planners, architects and artists to provide public art of the highest quality; and

WHEREAS ...

During the period March 19 through April 30, 1980 the Institute of Contemporary Art at the University of Pennsylvania will focus on Philadelphia's public art in a multi-media show, and will publish a map locating the sculpture derived through the Fine Arts Ordinance:

Now, Therefore ...

I, William J. Green, Mayor of the City of Philadelphia, do hereby proclaim Tuesday, March 18, 1980 as

PUBLIC ART DAY

in this city, do salute the new exhibition of the Institute of Contemporary Art, and do urge all the citizens to enjoy Philadelphia's art and this show to the fullest.

MAYOR

Given under my hand and the Seal of the City of Philadelphia, this eighteenth day of March, one thousand, nine hundred and eighty.

Urban Encounters

Institute of
Contemporary Art

University of
Pennsylvania

March 19–
April 30, 1980

Art

Architecture

Audience

This exhibition and catalogue have
been funded in part by the Design
Arts Program and Visual Arts Program of the National Endowment
for the Arts in Washington, D.C., a
federal agency, and the Pennsylvania Council on the Arts. A por-
tion of our general operating funds
for this fiscal year has been made
available through a grant from the
Institute of Museum Services, a
Federal agency in the Department
of Education, which offers operating and program support to the nation's museums.

Artists in the Exhibition

Stephen Antonakos

Jennifer Bartlett

Alexander Calder

Mark di Suvero

Rafael Ferrer

Richard Fleischner

Red Grooms

Lawrence Halprin

Lloyd Hamrol

Michael Heizer

Robert Indiana

Robert Irwin

Charles Moore

Robert Morris

Louise Nevelson

Isamu Noguchi

Claes Oldenburg

Eero Saarinen

Alan Sonfist

George Sugarman

Athena Tacha

Acknowledgments

"Urban Encounters: Art Architecture Audience" documents twenty-one selected sites in the United States that have been marked by an architect, landscape architect, painter, or sculptor during the past fifteen years. This catalogue reflects the great diversity of artworks and sites, reviews the nature of the public art enterprise, and suggests some guidelines to ease the entry of art into the public domain for future projects.

Assembling the exhibition required investigation beyond the usual curatorial parameters. Just as public art itself requires the participation of several "partners," I was aided by many people from diverse institutions and organizations. In searching for material inquiries were directed to city officials, building contractors, industrial fabricators, newspaper libraries, and many private citizens, who often had interesting documentation as a result of their encounter with artworks.

In initiating the exhibition Patricia Fuller of Art in Public Places, Visual Arts Program, National Endowment for the Arts (NEA), offered constant encouragement. I am deeply appreciative of her support. Julie Brown and Donald W. Thalacker of the General Services Administration (GSA) were also helpful in the generative stage of this project. Once the sites for the exhibition were determined, ICA's energetic staff, Amy Cohen, Paula Marincola, and Matthew McClain, were invaluable in locating appropriate material for the exhibition. We were assisted in this search by Olivia Georgia, Gerry Hazzard, Larry Hanson, Nicole Levin, Dee Mullen, Emily Pulitzer, Joyce Schwartz, and many others. William Baumann, Randy Dalton, and Donald Sullivan were ICA's expert installation crew, skillfully directed by John Taylor. William Wetmore served as our able security guard.

This catalogue has been greatly enriched by the essays of Lawrence Alloway, Nancy Foote, and Ian L. McHarg. Robin Kaplan and Barbara Schulman, work-study students; Mark Stivers, volunteer; and Ella Schaap, art historian and member of ICA's Advisory Board, contributed many hours of diligent research compiling the bibliography and list of 100 selected sites. They were aided by Cathy Conn and Stacey Paleologos of NEA, Julie Brown at GSA, and the staff of the Public Art Fund. The results of this research have been prepared for publication by ICA's staff members, Joan Horvath, Paula Marincola, and Karen Merkle Trosino. Michele Steege has served as our very capable editor. Jerome Cloud is responsible for the lucid design of the catalogue.

The ICA acknowledges with deep appreciation the support of the Design Program and Visual Arts Program of the National Endowment for the Arts, which made the exhibition and catalogue a reality. Marilyn L. Steinbright generously enabled us to publish a map locating Philadelphia's public art since 1959, the year that Philadelphia became the first United States city to adopt a one percent law for art. The Honorable William J. Green, Mayor of Philadelphia, proclaimed the opening date of this exhibition—March 18, 1980—"Philadelphia Public Sculpture Day." Members of ICA's Advisory Board offered steadfast encouragement throughout the project. There are a multitude of lenders to this exhibition, and I am very grateful to all of them.

My greatest appreciation goes to the architects, landscape architects, painters, and sculptors represented in the exhibition, who chose to create works for public spaces. Their pioneering efforts have deposited the legacy of urban encounters which inspired this exhibition and catalogue.

Janet Kardon
Director
Institute of
Contemporary Art

Contents

Street Wise/Street Foolish

Janet Kardon

Public art is not a style or a movement, but a compound social service based on the premise that public well-being is enhanced by good art, and that good art means work by advanced artists thrust into the public domain. We have as yet no satisfactory definition of public art. In the context of this exhibition, public art is defined as works in urban spaces through which people may pass, pause, gather or enact a variety of social activities. Public art by painters, sculptors, architects, and landscape designers is included. The work might be a mural or a single piece of sculpture created for a specific site, a complete site design, or part of a larger scheme. Such work may involve alteration, even reconstruction of the site, and such modifications may in themselves constitute the piece. Site specific work in remote areas is not, according to this definition, public art.

As a codified genre in this country, public art is about fifteen years old, if we mark the beginning with Picasso's model for the Chicago Civic Center, conceived in 1965 and installed in 1967. Today, surveying the sites marked with public art and the rather turbulent histories attached to many of the works, what are we to conclude? This exhibition and catalogue are not designed to provide final answers, but rather to focus the questions, identify the mistakes, and analyze some of the successes. Perhaps they may help remove some of the esthetic and administrative obstacles encountered with every worthwhile public art project.

The prervious efflorescence of public art—murals, photography, and sculpture—was associated with the Works Project Administration (WPA) between 1933 and 1943. The present activity—government and private—does not match that precedent in numbers or geographic distribution. Both modes of funding, proceeding from vastly different premises, have generated many works of quality. The WPA's artworks, funded to give artists employment, have had a somewhat fugitive existence.[1] No community asked for them. No rationale of subject or style attended their creation beyond the self-defined needs of the participating artists. The works in this exhibition, however, are based on several more sharply focused needs: the demands of a community to mark a space or of a corporation to enhance its image as a patron; and a process designed to choose quality works and introduce the public to recent esthetic developments. This catalogue lists one-hundred projects felt to be reasonable successes; the exhibition isolates twenty-one examples I consider to be especially important. Such works exemplify the range of responses from the makers of public art to the demands placed on them. The thesis of this exhibition is that while the public art area remains confused and its issues are undefined, sufficient good work has been made to give us some guidelines for the future. In the broadest sense public art is now the major arena in which democratic ideas and esthetic elitism attempt to come to terms with each other. Why is it proving so difficult?

The overriding issue of public art is one hardly noticed in the museum spaces where advanced art is shown to a self-selected public: realism. In no other area of art activity does the public's "right to recognize" the subject, content, and meaning of an artwork apply with such force. It is a misunderstood instinct. The tradition of advanced art is mainly one of abstraction. There is a basic incompatibility between the concepts of space generated by the modern movement and those invoked by traditional realism (realism here is defined as anthropomorphic, "humanistic" realism, not the "ideal" realities which modernism has sometimes pursued). The space of abstraction is a different space. Its gravitational rules, its metaphors, illusions, and purities are far from the everyday space in which the realist figure stands.[2] Realist figures do not disturb the space they share with the viewer. Larger than life,

Eero Saarinen
Jefferson National Expansion Memorial, 1965
St. Louis, Missouri
facing west

*Jefferson National
Expansion Memorial*

usually elevated, assuming postures from the heroic to the typical, they offer reassuring standards. That tradition in the 19th and early 20th centuries—the war memorials and celebrations of civic virtue—exemplifies qualities we may have overlooked. The huge abstract sculpture, which celebrates the fact of art before all else, is a threatening experience for a public who finds it without rationale, motive, or beauty. The way the abstract artwork relates to the space of the passer-by is one key to the negative reception that has become a kind of certificate of merit among modern artists. It redefines space in a way that is sensed rather than understood; it unsettles perceptions and does not reassure the viewer with an easily shared idea or subject.

Forms of abstract allegory with such themes as "flight," "motion," and "fire" find some acceptance. Our single greatest work of postwar sculpture, Saarinen's St. Louis Arch—a complex, brilliantly designed parabola—owes its present unanimous acceptance to the idea through which it purveys its real sculptural meaning. Referred to as "the gateway of the West," it flatters civic self-importance and just as surely rolls our eye through its hoop from every part of the city. The phrases recently used by Roland Barthes for the Eiffel Tower serve this work just as well: "the great ascensional dream"[3] . . . that "attracts meaning."[4] Without this key—an idea that gives the pedestrian's imagination some access to the work—abstract work is often felt to be a personal insult. Yet those responsible for creating, funding, and carrying through such projects often are astonished by such a basic

human response. The upper-middle-class attitude is that art is its own justification, as is philanthropy. This attitude, the fruit of higher education and social sophistication, is not that of the majority of passers-by. Such works insult the pedestrian doubly. They come from a special environment supported by the upper class—the museum, the artist's studio, the gallery—and because of their origin they remain opaque to the pedestrian's native understanding. There is a hidden class struggle behind the rumblings that accompany the public art enterprise.

It should not be assumed, however, that I entertain illusions about the general public's level of intelligence or taste, or that its opinions are to be blindly trusted. There is little historical evidence that the public ever produced a fine work of public art. It has generally been, as a recent symposium agreed,[5] the act of a single patron who donated the work to the public, who then got used to it. "No public has ever asked for public art; there is no demand for it," according to one of the participants at that symposium.[6]

The role of perceptual habits in facilitating the entry of a work into a community has not received enough attention. The public seems to develop a visual pact with its surroundings, a familiarity that resists change, no matter how beneficial or ideal the new intrusion may be—whether housing project, civic building,

City of Grand Rapids sanitation truck painted with
"La Grande Vitesse" logo

View of Vandenberg Plaza
Grand Rapids
facing west

Alexander Calder
"La Grande Vitesse," 1969
Grand Rapids, Michigan
facing west

or work of art. In sensing how the building, or the work of art relates to them, their instinct is acute. Members of the public seem to read accurately the attitudes implicit in the forms and functions of a building or artwork. In time, even the most intractable of public facilities is mobilized by human occupancy. This process is aided by the kind of wit, patience, and cynicism that the public displays towards the remote instigators of decisions they are expected to live with. All these are, I believe, important aspects of any discussion of public art. They are among the most misunderstood—if they are identified at all.

The reasons for the present activity in the public area have been often stated. Postwar urban planning intruded on organic downtown spaces, developed over decades, with new blueprinted spaces having little intimacy, scale, or grace. At the same time a growing sense of civic pride in smaller cities desired the mark that public art—or a fountain—offered (the public's instinct here is good; water is a wonderful material, and

a fountain has a glamour the western public has recognized for five centuries). There was also a new availability of funds, announced by the government adventure that began with Calder's *"La Grande Vitesse"* in Grand Rapids, Michigan in 1967.[7] New technology allowed large scale steel sculpture to be produced at reasonable cost.[8] The esthetics of the sixties—the abandonment of the pedestal, the discovery of the floor, interest in a larger scale, the influence of constructivism, and some minimalists' interest in industrial fabrication—favored the outdoor move to parks and plazas.

The conditions for the first phase of the public art venture were present. More than enlargement, however, was needed to procure suitable outdoor scale, since the move from the studio to the plaza brought with it the context of the studio, and did little to meet the needs of outdoor space or the public that would use these spaces. Most works remained self-contained and self-referential, however excellent they might be as art. The point became obvious that their status as good art, as judged by the art community according to its closed system of values, was only one of the needed factors for success outdoors.

Other problems also surfaced. In the downtown renewal areas that provided the stage for the presentation of large constructivist/minimalist objects, exhibiting a range of geometric calisthenics, such works were usually introduced after the architectural fact. Corporations and government panels sometimes selected what turned out to be a fine work doubtfully sited in the overall plan, becoming a specimen of a new genre of architectural jewelry. Constructivist/minimalist work

Michael Heizer
Adjacent Against Upon, 1976
Seattle, Washington
facing northeast and south

Mark di Suvero
Under Sky/One Family, 1979
Baltimore, Maryland
facing west

often politely echoed international style buildings, thus enhancing the artist-architect collaboration on a somewhat doubtful basis. Biomorphic curves that could play against the international style grid were virtually proscribed. There was also an element of artist-architect competition, beginning with sixties minimalism, and witnessed in many exhibitions on scale and size. This at times resulted in new museums which competed with their contents (the forerunner of this was Wright's Guggenheim Museum; other examples are Pei's Everson Museum and Breuer's Whitney Museum). Some museums began to site sculpture in their grounds as a "marquee" for their collections.

In the seventies as post-modern architecture examined its options, the overlap—and competition between—artist and architect blurred many issues. No examination of the assumptions and roles of the two fields or of how they might gainfully cooperate exists. When two fields and two traditions are superimposed, surely there can be intelligent analysis from some quarter to calculate the profits and losses of the merger. In the sixties, however, post-modern architecture was not yet the design choice for public buildings; most were indifferent, third generation international style. Public sculpture was often a cosmetic attempt to mitigate the effects of poor architectural solutions.

"Urban Encounters: Art Architecture Audience" contains diverse materials relating to the work: maquettes, drawings, photographs, site plans, correspondence, videotapes, and slides. Twenty-one public spaces in cities across the United States have been selected. Projects for these spaces include the full spectrum of possibilities as revealed to us by the sixties and seventies: monolithic sculpture, often conceived with the expectancy that it could reside amiably on any plaza; sites

designed by the guiding hand of the landscape architect or architect; and site-oriented artworks incorporate their surroundings through a variety of devices.

The settings of the twenty-one sites reveal a diverse inventory. Claes Oldenburg's and George Sugarman's works are located on preexisting city plazas. City parks provide a naturalistic backdrop for works by Richard Fleischner, Lawrence Halprin, Robert Irwin, Alan Sonfist, and Athena Tacha. Mark di Suvero, Michael Heizer, and Eero Saarinen have sited their works near water. Rafael Ferrer's sculpture stands on a vacant lot in a transitional area. Charles Moore, Louise Nevelson, and Isamu Noguchi designed encapsulated city spaces. The indoor sites include a swimming pool ceiling by Stephen Antonakos, a lobby wall in an office building by Jennifer Bartlett, a museum bookstore by Red Grooms, and a basketball court floor by Robert Indiana.

The exhibition marks what I consider a period of transition from the studio work, suitably enlarged and sited, to site-oriented work. It also provides an opportunity to compare the work of painters and sculptors with some urban spaces created by architects and landscape designers.

In selecting these works I have sought to provide exemplary occasions not only in terms of the artwork, but in terms of the processes that preceded and succeeded it. We now know that negotiating an artwork into the public consciousness involves far more than we had hitherto thought. Several questions surround the entire process—the first one being, "Should there be public art at all?" If we reply positively, we need to be fully informed on the physical and social setting; the nature of the patronage; the appropriateness of the contemplated artwork; and how it can be made less of a hostile interloper on a familiar scene. There is, we must understand, a time-consuming art involved in the

Jennifer Bartlett
Swimmers Atlanta, 1979
Atlanta, Georgia

See color plate pg. 40

14 psychological siting of the work, and anything that helps us understand this process is valuable. The habitual arguments may not be the most effective, i.e., that the work represents the best art being done today, that its message is primarily artistic, that the artist is respected nationally since museums have shown the work and critics have praised it, and that major collectors seek the artists' products. Museums, critics, collectors, and the judgment of out-of-town experts (the national reputation) is a kind of elitist persuasion that remains remote from the common sense of the public.

There is work that should not, in my opinion, be adapted to public use. It is simply too involved in its own interior esthetic monologue. The public is persuaded when the work can be perceived as symbolizing some public concern or dream; when the artist, seen in person, is not overtly objectionable or hostile, and is perceived as a worker and problem solver. Entry is facilitated when the public perceives the work as performing some useful task, whether it is simply that of shade and seating, or something even remotely associated with the sense of leisure. To be guided through space in a way that rewards the passer-by is of prime value to the public. The artwork must be seen as part of a socializing process in which the public in turn adapts the work for its own purposes—a fortunate accident that resulted in the case of the Grand Rapids' Calder.

The modernist tradition, it can now be said, has not provided us with much latitude for public artworks. Its formalist pursuits have depreciated to the point where they are of little public interest and its ability to communicate in any meaningful way with a broad group has been limited. Its attempts to celebrate an event tend to ignore the event in everything but the title.

Robert Indiana
MECCA, 1977
Basketball Court
Milwaukee, Wisconsin

See color plate pg. 40

Most works of public art, having come down from the traditional pedestal in an overdue esthetic adventure, are ill-sited and ill-served by the places in which they find themselves, and people frequently walk past them with indifference. The works documented in this exhibition survive, I believe, rather more happily in meeting the obligatory double-standard: performing the reasonable function of satisfying enlightened taste; and making themselves acceptable on some basis to the public.

The exhibition made manifest the clear distinction between architect/planner and artist, to the detriment of the latter. Architects and planners do not share the uncompromising attitude and isolation of art-making which is a liability in public discourse. The artists' conception of their role, if they are going to enter the public dialogue, may need revision. The tradition of collaboration between artist and city official is limited. In site-specific work especially, artists enter an arena in which, as a group, they are at a disadvantage.

We have come near the end of the cycle that began around 1965 when manufacturing technology and constructivist/minimalist esthetics together made large scale public work possible and of interest to several artists. The understanding of public space, of perceptual habits, and of the territorial impetus of vision itself are still to be brought into alignment with something other than the rather suspect virtue of quality as an isolated value. Space itself has changed. It has been demystified and rendered placeless, and this has not encouraged the elements of rhetoric any successful work of public art must have. The commemorative idea—the celebration of a person or event or achievement—has not yet been superseded as the key to public art. To forget this is to attempt a discourse from positions that optimize the possibility for misunderstanding. When initiating the exhibition, my assumptions were those of any curator interested in establishing a productive liaison between advanced art and the public; and in evaluating the museum's role in such collaboration, including its educational responsibilities. I must admit that after assembling and mounting the exhibition, my doubts about the nature of public art, as presently defined, have been encouraged as much as resolved.

1. The most notable example is the Arshile Gorky mural for the Newark Airport, rediscovered by Ruth Bowman. Please see the exhibition catalogue, Ruth Bowman, *Murals Without Walls: Arshile Gorky's Aviation Murals Rediscovered*, The Newark Museum, Newark, New Jersey, 1978.

2. Linda Nochlin, "The Realist Criminal and the Abstract Law," *Art in America*, September-October, 1973, pp. 54-61.

3. Roland Barthes, *The Eiffel Tower and Other Mythologies*, Hill and Wang, a New York division of Farrar, Straus and Giroux, Inc., 1979, p. 7.

4. *Ibid.*, p. 5.

5. "Earthworks: Land Reclamation as Sculpture," a series of symposiums, proposals and completed earthworks sponsored by the King County Arts Commission and the King County Department of Public Works, Seattle, Washington, July 31-August 18, 1978.

6. *Ibid.*, a comment by Mary Miss on August 18, 1978, at one of the symposiums.

7. The first National Endowment for the Arts matching grant for public art was awarded to the City of Grand Rapids, Michigan. The amount was $45,000. In 1980, $760,000 has been allocated for Art in Public Spaces. Thus far, 238 works have been funded by the program. The General Services Administration funds projects for federal buildings. See Donald W. Thalacker, *The Place of Art in the World of Architecture*, Chelsea House Publishers in association with R.R. Bowker Company, New York, London, 1980.

8. Lippincott Industrial Fabrication, one of the most useful facilities for fabrication of large scale works, was founded in 1963.

Problems of Iconography and Style

Lawrence Alloway

Despite "the triumph of art for the public," as Elizabeth Gilmore Holt put it,[1] public art itself is not ascendant. The kind of art that triumphed of course is the personally based art distributed by galleries and museums. The term public art denotes works that are to be seen outside the special viewing that the exhibition system provides. There is a great difference between seeing works of art in places designed to show them and seeing them accidentally, in the course of doing something else, on the edge of other activity. The public work is seen by an unspecialized public, diversified by age, sex, income, and race, whereas the public for art is pre-selected by the act of attending a museum, even more so by going to an art gallery.

After Napoleon became emperor, he generated a court art, a coordinated high style for clocks, furniture, painting, sculpture, and textiles. Within his domestic and ceremonial precincts, art provided a unified ambiance. Obviously there is no coordinated style now, nor any way to enforce one. Artists who work in public must do so without any prior assurance of social relevance. A public work of art enters the environment of artifacts, controllable in Napoleon's time, uncontrollable in ours. What does it mean for an artist's work to enter the environment of artifacts? It means to take part in the man-made landscape as it is shaped by architects and designers, by city ordinances and regional planning. Since the end of World War II, there have been two major developments in terms of the environment: one is a speedup of the process of deterioration; the other is the proliferation of redevelopment projects. These projects are numerous, but their impact is small in relation to the overall rate of man-induced entropy. The question is, what do artists contribute to these pockets of redevelopment? How should we judge their environmental awareness? There are few signs that artists recognize this opportunity, which is linked to their lack of interest in public art as different from art. Samuel Taylor Coleridge pointed out that "all languages perfect themselves by a gradual process of desynonymizing words originally equivalent."[2] Given the inconclusive state of the discussion of public art, it is inadequate to call everything that an artist does "art" without making an effort at more precise definitions.

Artists and critics are both equivocal about and resistant to the idea of public art. Take the case of Picasso's *Guernica*, incontestably a successful public work of art, more familiar to a broader audience than his "civilian" works. When questioned about the symbolism of his picture, Picasso said: "The public who looks at the picture must see in the horse and the bull symbols which they interpret as they understand them. There are some animals. That's all, so far as I'm concerned. It's up to the public to see what it wants to see."[3] He is talking ten years after doing the painting, but his words seem not to match the facts that the work was done in response to a specific event, the first "modern" air raid, and was intended for a specific destination, the Spanish pavilion of a world exhibition. He is in a sense pulling his picture back to the studio by denying the communicability of the work except as a *Picasso*. According to Clement Greenberg, "the explicit comment on an historical event offered in Picasso's *Guernica* does not make it necessarily a better or richer work than an utterly 'nonobjective' painting by Mondrian."[4] He argues that Picasso's attempt to expand cubism to "the museum and Michelangeloesque idea of a grand style"[5] flaws the work. Thus we have the artist removing the basis for an iconographical reading of his painting and a critic contending that the picture

Claes Oldenburg
Batcolumn, 1977
Chicago, Illinois
(not included in exhibition)

has been wrecked by its concessions to a public rhetoric. These positions are typical of the problems that stand in the way of formulating a theory of public art. Artists are reluctant to comply with legible iconographic systems, and critics are more interested in syntactical integrity than semantic content.

The incidence of outdoor sculpture, the aspect of public art with which this exhibition is concerned, increased in the 1970s, partly owing to a federal program, partly owing to the private sector. The National Endowment for the Arts' (NEA) Art in Public Places program, originally a Kennedy proposal, was revived at a time when the General Services Administration (GSA) was doing a lot of building for the government. A small percentage of a building's construction costs was available for art if the architects requested it. They informed the GSA who contacted the NEA which convened a panel of experts to select artists. Among the works achieved by this route are Chicago's Alexander Calder, *Flamingo*, and Claes Oldenburg, *Batcolumn*. Corporate patronage was also active, as in the case of Jean Dubuffet's *Group of Four Trees* in New York sponsored by the Chase Manhattan Bank and Isamu Noguchi's *Portal* at the Justice Center in Cleveland, Ohio, underwritten by the George Gund Foundation.

One remembers the difficulties that artists experienced in trying to deal with Bicentennial themes, lacking an iconography compatible with their formal interests. Louise Nevelson's sculpture in the Courthouse and Federal Building in Philadelphia is entitled *Bicentennial Dawn*, but calling it that does not make it so. In fact the work is a fully characteristic Nevelson,

and its place in the sequence of her work overcomes any external signification. Barnett Newman's *Broken Obelisk* in Houston, Texas, is dedicated to Martin Luther King, Jr. The sculpture is one of an edition of three, and the others do not have the dedication, which was added by the owner, John D. Menil, with the artist's consent. If meaning is so volatile, one wonders what is being commemorated in such public sculptures. The answer would seem to be: the artists. The subject is their styles, in larger examples than usual, displaced from the usual system of distribution. The innovative aspect of public art often seems to be located more in the commissioning agencies than in the artists' work.

Public art seems bound by a surprise-free requirement, because artists have to have reached a certain level of proven skill and reputation to qualify for a commission and they remain, prudently, within the limits of the work that got them the job. For the most part artists tend to do on a larger scale what they have already done or to realize projects that they conceived earlier but were delayed by fabrication costs. This does not mean that the taxpayers are being cheated in the federal projects. Barbara Rose has pointed out, in response to this complaint by Senator Proxmire (D. Wisconsin), that "no sculptor has made a dime of profit on a GSA public commission,"[6] referring specifically to the *Batcolumn*. It is true that the grants are tight, but it also is true that artists have not done much with them.

Barnett Newman
Broken Obelisk, 1971
Houston, Texas
(not included in exhibition)

Jean Dubuffet
Group of Four Trees, 1972
New York, New York
(not included in exhibition)

Claes Oldenburg
Clothespin, 1976
Philadelphia, Pennsylvania
facing east

They have neither innovated in the forms of the man-made environment nor extended the audience for art appreciably.

Rose described Oldenburg's *Clothespin* in Centre Square, Philadelphia, as "humanizing an environment of official skyscrapers,"[7] but this is not really how it works. The site represents a conventional use of sculpture according to the principle of contrast: fat compared to thin, spiky to smooth, or as here, rusty to new. It has been a cliche of 20th century siting, ever since Mies van der Rohe placed a Maillol bronze of a hefty woman among the lean, right-angled planes of his architecture. Picturesque contrast is also the principle of siting at the Federal Building and U.S. Courthouse Plaza, Baltimore, Maryland where George Sugarman's curling planes of color are set against the regular pattern of the building. Nevelson's personages in New York, *Shadows and Flags*, are Stygian black compared to the rough textures of the surrounding buildings. In these cases, as so often in public situations, sculpture is what is different from architecture. Sculptors may regard this as preserving their aesthetic autonomy, but in fact the sculpture recedes to a secondary place within the containing architectural framework.

There have been several cases in which certain groups have not been grateful for the deposit of art in spaces they use; their reactions have ranged from residents' demurrals about sculptures set in the central division of Park Avenue, New York, to intense controversy, as in the case of Sugarman's Baltimore piece. Such occurrences are usually interpreted by the art community as Philistine resistance to improvement, but improvement for whom? A known space suddenly receives a public work of art: is it a gift or an invasion? If a gift, whose? Ideological suspicions encourage resistance. Often the work is viewed as a kind of UFO, strange because it exemplified the donor's taste, not that of the recipients. Urban space is a social experience, and the sudden appearance of unknown objects encroaches on behavior as well as on taste.

Some of the problems afflicting public art, but not art in general can be summed up now. 1. There is a widespread lack of interest among artists, which shows in their poor record of responsiveness to sites and in their indifference to a shared iconography. 2. Owing to their specialization, artists' contributions to the environment of artifacts have been reduced in significance to the building of personal memorials. 3. There is also in the general public an irregular level of art education: it is high enough to support *more* public art, but still includes considerable distrust of artists (and the institutions for which they work). There are ideological as well as esthetic reasons for resistance to

George Sugarman
Baltimore Federal, 1978
Baltimore, Maryland
(detail)

See color plate pg. 45

Cecile Abish
Renaissance Fix, 1979
Installation at Hudson River Museum
Yonkers, New York
(not included in exhibition)

public art. This is engendered, for example, when abstract art forms become identified as corporate logos.

The notion that public sculpture should be object-centered has prevented artists from contributing to the formation of the urban continuum. Despite their occasional demands for fuller consultation by architects, few artists have demonstrated the conceptual ability to take advantage of it if it were forthcoming.[8] It is significant that once big pieces by, say, Oldenburg and Clement Meadmore, Noguchi, and Sugarman are put in outdoor settings, they reveal similarities. In the gallery or museum, stylistic differences are crucial, but in the street, the works of art represent a single level of cultivation compared to all the surrounding hardware.

Sculptures that lead in another direction include works in Michigan, New York, and Ohio. There is Robert Morris' *Grand Rapids Project*, a big hard-top X on the side of a hill in a park; it can be viewed as a sign (X marks the spot) or traversed like a path. Alan Sonfist's *Time Landscape* on an 18,000 square-foot site in downtown Manhattan is a contoured area planted with vegetation indigenous to the island before colonization. Athena Tacha's *Streams* is a step-like construc-

tion of blocks following the contours of a small hill in a park; its geometric elements are a fluid sequence.[9] Ambiance-responsiveness rather that monumentality characterizes all three pieces (though Morris preserves his customary touch of oppression). These works function on the ground plane rather than above it. One thinks too of Carl Andre, Barry Le Va, and Cecile Abish whose recently completed indoor floor piece, *Renaissance Fix*, could be extrapolated to public scale.[10] Another alternative is what might be called the sculpture of habitations,[11] works that deal with enclosure in fantasied or occupiable form: houses, walls, tents, vaults, corridors, or trenches. Among the artists who work in this extensive, multi-centered form are Alice Adams, Siah Armajani, Alice Aycock, Donna Dennis, Harriet Feigenbaum, Rafael Ferrer, and Mary Miss. There is a spatial imagination, a sense of architecture and play, that is substantially different from object-centered sculpture.

facing southwest

(detail)

Louise Nevelson
Shadows and Flags
(Louise Nevelson Park), 1978
New York, New York

(detail)

20   Public sculpture used to be able to draw on the poetry of institutions as a source of resonant iconography. Equestrian monuments, of which Falconet's *Peter the Great* in Leningrad is the climax, celebrate absolute authority; later, seated figures in modern suits symbolize parliamentary or democratic authority. In the absence of agreed-on canons of leadership, however, what can the artist do now? Lacking political references, we are in need of a public art that rests on another basis, that of the shareable present. Participation may take the place of unusable iconography or style-oriented monumentality. This means more than exercise in a jungle gym. It would involve entering the sculpture's space, looking outward from within the work, completing it physically by one's presence. Environmental sculpture would be less assertive of the identity of artists, a matter of small concern to the general public. Though the structures would be stable, they would be subject to variable use and occupation. Such sculpture would relate more to leisure than to commemoration, and more to participation than to an inventory of the solid forms of late abstract art.

Robert Morris
Grand Rapids Project, 1974
Grand Rapids, Michigan
(not included in exhibition)

Alan Sonfist
Time Landscape, A Reconstruction of a Pre-Colonial Forest, 1977
New York, New York
facing south

1. Elizabeth Gilmore Holt, ed., *The Triumph of Art for the Public*, Anchor Press, Garden City, New York, 1979.

2. Samuel Taylor Coleridge, *Biographia Literaria, II*. Quoted in Tomas Maldonado, *Design, Nature, and Revolution: Toward a Critical Ecology*, Harper & Row, New York, 1972. pp. 64-65. The concept of the artifact environment is taken from Maldonado, p. 79.

3. Dore Ashton, *Picasso on Art: A Selection of Views*, Viking Press, New York, 1972, p. 129.

4. Clement Greenberg, *Art and Culture*, Beacon Press, Boston, 1961, p. 134.

5. *Ibid.*, p. 63.

6. Barbara Rose, "Public Art's Big Hit," *Vogue*, July 1977, pp. 118, 145.

7. *Ibid.*

8. An exception is Robert Smithson, in "Towards the Development of an Air Terminal Site," *The Writings of Robert Smithson*, Nancy Holt, ed., New York University Press, New York, 1979, pp. 41-47.

9. See, Grand Rapids Art Museum, Robert Morris, "Grand Rapids Project," 1975; Alan Sonfist, "Natural Phenomena as Public Monuments," *Tracks 3*, 1-2, Spring 1977, pp. 44-47; Athena Tacha, "Rhythm as Form," *Landscape Architecture*, May 1978, pp. 196-205 (vol. 68).

10. "Supershow," a traveling exhibition organized by Independent Curators, Inc., 1979.

11. For a partial survey, see *Dwellings* exhibition catalogue, University of Pennsylvania, Institute of Contemporary Art, Philadelphia, 1978, organized by Suzanne Delehanty, essay by Lucy R. Lippard.

Three Essays on Urban Space

Ian L. McHarg

Generations of American architects who have toured Europe have been beguiled by *piazza* and *place*, enriched Kodak by their discovery, and returned with the firm resolve to enhance the American scene with this enchanting European image. No other European import, save the sidewalk cafe, has been so ardently admired and emulated.

In vain. American private space is relatively luxurious since it is less prodigal than in Europe; continental public space compensates for the deficiencies in private space. The nobles of Renaissance Italy and France were prepared to make greater investments in urban amenity than are merchants or municipalities in capitalist countries. Perhaps too, centuries of tradition in the design of public urban space resulted in skills which cannot be achieved by insistence. Of course, the European *piazza* was not only used for meeting and discourse but for entertainment and pageantry as well. These are provided in surfeit by television, movies, telephone, and more in modern America.

Whatever the reasons, the transatlantic passage has proven to be impossible. The animated, populated *piazza* with rich material, pattern and pigeons, fountains and sculpture, sidewalk cafes and bouquets of trees, have remained obdurately continental, and the pale shadows that have been realized in the United States are arid, contrived, self-conscious, and often empty, where sculpture seeks to provide the animation that people will not supply. The single contribution of the American plaza has been the interception of high velocity winds, which descend the faces of towering office buildings in great turbulence to the discomfiture of pedestrians.

So San Marco, Navona, Siena, San Pietro, del Popolo, and San Gimignano stay at home, and in Philadelphia, Denver, Hartford, Fort Worth, Boston, and New York, a succession of vaunted urban spaces fail to make the city any more humane. This is particularly tragic in New York where zoning appealed to avarice by permitting higher buildings if the plan provided open space. But these spaces have contributed little to urban delight; they are indeed indictments. There are two New York exceptions. One, to be discussed elsewhere, is the magic Museum of Modern Art garden, a marvelous oasis, a gift of Philip Johnson. The other, smaller still, is the Paley Park by the landscape architects Zion and Breen.

I could begin with no better example than the Paley Park, located on 53rd Street between 5th and Madison Avenues. Photographs cannot possibly convey the turbulence, human and mechanical, which provides the context. The inordinate success of this project lies in the contrast it provides—an eddy of peace just off a tempestuous stream of people and automobiles, a cacophony climaxed by clarions of police and ambulance.

Only four broad steps divide this little garden room from the sidewalk, but on climbing them one enters another world—shade and dappled light from a bosquet of trees, cool and calm. Within, one becomes conscious of another sound, of cascading water, a benign white noise that overwhelms the urban clamor. Tables, chairs, flower boxes complete the scene. Its success provides what is needed: the chance to leave the sidewalk treadmill, the opportunity to sit in peace, the sanctuary of shade, and the cooling sound of falling water—all this in so little space, so understated, yet with such moving power.

Lawrence Halprin's *Lovejoy Plaza* fountain in Portland, Oregon, is also a water poem, but the scale is vastly enlarged. This consists of cascades and waterfalls, which invite exuberant participation and receive it in full measure.

The fountain exploits a sloping site. At the upper level a wide planted berm separates the plaza from the sidewalk. The plaza evolves into a system of pools and interpenetrating planes that lie above a system of waterfalls. These, seen from below, provide a stage background for a pool with islands. This is overlooked by a stepped amphitheatre ascending to the lower forecourt.

Zion and Breen
Paley Park, 1967
New York, New York
(not included in exhibition)

These bald words convey none of the energy of water and people which animate this place on any decent day. It is a place, an event, a cynosure, and a celebration.

Wherein lies its success? Well first, its exuberance. The environment is not calm, calculated, contrived, and, as is so often the case, arid. It invites active participation and receives it. Next, its evocation— mountains and waterfalls—are a real background to Portland; the vocabulary is evocative of the natural context. But most of all the design is a stage in which all participate and contribute. This is its unique success. No other American plaza, to the best of my knowledge, receives this degree of use, pride, and approbation. This is its best testament.

Halprin's as yet unrealized Franklin Delano Roosevelt Memorial for Washington, D.C., is to be located on a nodal point on the L'Enfant plan, which was identified as a site for a memorial on the McMillan plan and allocated as the site for the F.D.R. Memorial by Congress in 1957. Once mud flats on the Potomac, the site was reclaimed late in the 19th century and developed with the Cherry Walk to the river.

This may be one of the most important public commissions of this century, and the selection committee should be congratulated for selecting Halprin— unquestionably the most talented living landscape architect.

Normally criticism of projects must rely on plans, perspectives, and models, but in this instance a much richer body of evidence was made available. Glen Fleck, long-time colleague of Charles Eames in making documentary films, worked with Halprin to create a film depicting the experience to be presented in the Memorial. The process of film making became a significant element in Halprin's design process. As one who worked with Mr. Fleck in making a movie of a projected environmental park in Iran, I, too, can testify to the extraordinary value of film as a design tool.

Halprin's design supports my assertion of his remarkable talents. The Memorial is, in mood, a garden, exploiting mature existing elms and cherry trees; but in experience it is a processional that leads the visitor on a thousand-foot walk through four major spaces, each devoted to a significant aspect of Roosevelts life.

Within the larger context of the bordering Tidal Basin and the canopy of trees, the major unifying element is a meandering granite wall, sometimes of dressed stone, sometimes of massive rough blocks. It is this wall that defines one side of the processional and the sequence of spaces. The other side, in most areas, employs planting for definition.

(detail of fountain)

Lawrence Halprin
Lovejoy Plaza, 1965
Portland, Oregon

(detail of fountain)

Upon the wall are incised memorable statements by F.D.R. and Leonard Baskin's reliefs of the Great Seal of the United States, and F.D.R. as Commander in Chief. Other sculptures were commissioned from Neil Estern, Robert Graham, and George Segal.

The granite wall is one unifying element; water is the second. It appears in various expressions, leading to the final experience: the great water garden feature. Here the visitor enters the room defined by tall trees where the unifying wall becomes a system of waterfalls. This is a superb work—strong, quiet, dignified, moving, and contemplative. May it be built.

The three projects which I have selected have been designed by landscape architects, and this may well explain their success. It certainly goes far toward explaining their mode of expression and their commitment to an evocation of nature. The content of the design is the gift that nature's benison can give to the city of man. All artists employ symbolic formal language, but the landscape architect selects nature as the subject and source of materials. While the materials of painter, sculptor, and architect are inert and often very plastic, the living materials employed by the landscape architect are, at least, insistent upon the preconditions for survival. They are alive. But the initial point is the most powerful: the landscape architect does not have to search for a subject to communicate. His subject is nature and natural systems, and this provides his palette. His works are an evocation of nature in man's world.

The success of these landscape architects may well explain why the European plaza has not transplanted well. The European need, which at least historically was for public space for discourse and entertainment, may well be quite different from the American need. As the migration to the suburb and the country shows, it may well be that the image of nature is the greatest perceived deficiency in the modern city, and providing this may be the key to success. This suggests not a transplanted European plaza, but a native American one, responsive to modern needs, responsive to place and people.

Lawrence Halprin
Model for *F.D.R. Memorial*
Washington, D.C.
(not included in exhibition)

Sightings on Siting

Nancy Foote

The 1970s spawned a diffuse pluralism in art and a vague, ill-defined critical vocabulary. Ironically, though not surprisingly, a decade in which art often relied heavily on language failed to establish clearly its terms of discourse. Take, for example, the subject of this exhibition: we speak of "public art," "Earthworks," "installations," "environmental sculpture," "site-specific works," "sited sculpture," "projects," "land reclamation." These are some of the labels that have attached themselves to the vast arena of '70s art activity which falls into the category of "not painting." It is, of course, a lot easier to invent a term than to apply old ones with accuracy and clarity. Coining a label is also a time-honored strategy for proclaiming that you are doing something new. It is, in fact, an anti-critical tactic, glossing over precisely *how* something is new, and perhaps more important, how it isn't.

Rosalind Krauss has argued convincingly that much of the art under consideration here should not be called sculpture at all.[1] In her view, the notion of sculpture, wedded to the monument, was undermined by the "sitelessness" that characterizes modernist sculpture. The present activity, for her, falls between "not landscape" and "not architecture." I think she makes an important point. However, I am less interested here in worrying about a definition of sculpture than in investigating the various claims being made in the name of recent outdoor art, bearing with it its jumbled collection of epithets.

There is nothing new about the idea of siting a sculpture. Until the disappearance of the monument, it was taken for granted that a sculpture was sited, both physically and ideologically. Physical siting disappeared when works began to be made for museums and galleries—"neutral" spaces.[2] This new neutrality of site coincided with the disappearance of symbolic content brought about by abstract art. Monuments on pedestals, often embellished with narrative friezes, had openly displayed their content, in fact counted on it for their meaning. Their audience was the general public, not the art connoisseur. Their physical site was the territory of that public; their ideological "site," its collective consciousness. The failure of much recent monumental abstract sculpture is that while it physically inhabits public territory, it retains its modernist aloofness. Claes Oldenburg may have been the first contemporary artist to realize this; his proposed colossal monuments comment wittily (albeit backhandedly) not only on the problems of physical siting, but on the importance of public recognition of popular, indeed banal, content.

As heirs to both "public art" and first-generation Earthworks, artists of the '70s have responded to these problems with several quasi-solutions. Some of their works are site-specific; others make that claim. All are, to varying degrees, anti-formal; most use natural materials and hand-built construction. They are concerned more with the situation given them than with producing an object. With siting as the new focus, these artists look to different models from those of their constructivist-oriented predecessors. The lines of Nazca, the standing stones and burial mounds of neolithic Britain and Ireland, pre-Columbian architecture, to name a few, have come under close scrutiny. But their connection to the '70s enterprise, while undisputed, remains problematic. These phenomena were probably site-specific, though we cannot be sure; their original *raisons d'être* are now lost to us. But '70s allusions to them through conscious quotation may derive as much from modernism's exploitation of the archeological model as from genuine understanding of their religious and social origins. These ancient sources were, after all, not made as "art."

Setting aside the similar characteristics of 1970s outdoor art, how do individual works differ? Some works are truly site-specific (Robert Irwin refers to these as "site-determined"); others, though more closely integrated with their sites than the placed object, are not. For a work to be site-specific, it must fully acknowledge its inalterable context, taking its cues from what is already there. Even making the work out of the materials of the site does not necessarily achieve this. Richard Fleischner's *Sod Maze*, 1974, is built into a lawn in Providence, Rhode Island, and cannot be moved without destroying it. However, since it could just as well be built on any lush, flat expanse of lawn, it is not really site-specific.

Fleischner's *Cow Island Project*, 1976-77, in Roger Williams Park in Providence, however, is. The setting is a two-acre island in a lake, separated from the shore by a narrow canal. Fleischner built a small footbridge across the canal which leads onto a rough, worn path extending up a low hill to the top of the island. Part way up, set into the ground across the path, a flat slab of pink granite serves as the threshold to the work. On top of the hill, sited between two oak trees, is a flat, open square consisting of six slabs of pink granite. From the square two long parallel bars of black granite extend along the ground down the other side of the hill toward the water. Thus bridge, existing path, threshold, trees, square, and bars combine to form the main axis of the piece—and the island. Two secondary axes, which pass roughly diagonally through the square, are established by additional markers off to the sides—a low black granite pillar on the left, a pink one on the right, and two pink slabs forming steps. This discreet interweaving of natural formal elements, each drawing attention to the properties of the other, annotates the space, while intruding only ever so slightly. It is a work connoting solitude and contemplation; one's perceptions must be sensitively tuned to receive its low-key signals.

Athena Tacha's *Streams*, 1975-76, in Oberlin, Ohio, also situated in a park, combines the elements of Fleischner's *Cow Island Project*—water, stone slabs, a hill—to very different ends. Here the hill forms the bank of Plum Creek, a small stream that flows through the park. Tacha, who ascribes her longtime fascination with staircases to visits to ancient sites on the Greek islands,[3] used cement blocks in various stacked arrangements to build a multi-tiered, random expanse of steps up the side of the hill. "Risers" and "treads" vary in size along a given level depending on the number of blocks used for a particular section. The steps are faced with sandstone; small, rough boulders punctuate divisions between the sections. The descending rhythms of the steps and the interruptions of the boulders echo the character of the stream below. The piece is meant to be climbed up or sat on; Tacha wants to call attention to the rhythms of walking, stepping, and climbing by throwing off one's accustomed stride.[4]

Lloyd Hamrol's *Log Ramps*, 1974, at the University of Western Washington in Bellingham, while not really site-specific in the sense of Fleischner or Tacha, still draws its audience in and makes fairly direct reference to the nature of its surroundings. The piece consists of four slanting triangular ramps, faced with logs, juxtaposed with each other, and angling up from the ground to form a low-roofed enclosure. One side faces a university building; the other turns out toward a pine forest

Richard Fleischner
Cow Island Project, 1978
Providence, Rhode Island

that might well have supplied its raw materials. Its private interior offers a respite from communal campus life; the rough-hewn logs of the outer surface allude to Washington's greatest natural resource—timber.

Theoretically, the same work can be site-specific or not, depending on its underlying premise. If, as Vincent Scully has suggested,[5] the Greek temples are oriented toward a specific element in the landscape, they become site-specific. But if they are merely oriented toward the east, are they still "sited"? Nancy Holt's recent work at the University of Western Washington and her earlier *Sun Tunnels* are positioned on their sites according to the compass points and the sunrise on the summer solstice respectively. They function only because of their specific placement within their sites, but they could be arranged in other locations to work in the same manner.

Alan Sonfist's *Time Landscape*, begun in 1969, is an 18,000-square-foot plot of land on the corner of La Guardia Place in New York which the artist has planted with shrubs, grasses, and trees indigenous to primeval Manhattan. Surrounded by a chain-link fence to protect it from the modern city, its overgrown frowziness and hummocky terrain comment on the artifice that characterizes even the city's "natural" areas. Olmstead's parks, planted with as many exotic flora as will with-

Athena Tacha
Streams, 1976
Oberlin, Ohio
facing southwest

stand the climate, are symphonic arrangements of nature. Sonfist's plot gives a hint of the uncultivated. It is certainly site-specific—in concept, at least—to the original island of Manhattan, if not to La Guardia Place, where it happens to be growing. Its existence, however, remains somewhat problematic. The fence, essential to its preservation, at the same time divorces it from its real site—the modern city (a little of which has managed to sneak in anyway, in the guise of beer cans and litter). While its poetic evocation of the past is appealing, its ability to function successfully in its location is questionable. Incidentally, it is also harder to define as "sculpture" than most '70s work. Robert Smithson was aware of the problems inherent in works like *Time Landscape*, raising the issue in his *Site/Non-Site* pieces. These small displacements of dirt, rocks, etc. are transported into the gallery. The gallery becomes the non-site, the aritist's comment on the neutral space created by modernist art for its own reception.

The Earthworks of the late '60s were anti-formal in concept, but their inaccessibility perpetuated a modernist diffidence, an alienation from the audience that has been disappearing in the '70s. Smithson, despite his many inaccessible projects, foresaw and advocated such a change, writing in the early '70s in favor of earth artists becoming involved in land reclamation.[6] In Seattle, Washington, in the summer of 1979, this aim was fulfilled. A major public project, organized by the Department of Public Works and the Seattle Arts Commission, and assisted by other local government agen-

cies, brought eight artists in to transform environmental eyesores—four old gravel pits, a creek with erosion problems, an ex-naval air station, a garbage landfill, and a strip along the airport runway uninhabitable because of noise pollution.[7] The sites are enormous; the artists were saddled with all sorts of extraesthetic problems from drainage to grade requirements to "cost effectiveness." The solutions range from the "public" (two park/picnic/recreation areas) to the "sculptural" (terraced gravel pits, built structures in the airport "ramble") to the "fantastic" (Dennis Oppenheim's proposal for the air station: *A Thought Collision Factory for Ghost Ships*). Most of these projects are still at the planning stage; it remains to be seen whether the enormous enthusiasms that generated the scheme will be able to carry through the hard-core realities of execution— fund-raising, politics, the building process itself. Another issue raised at the symposium kicking off the projects was: are artists being hired to cosmetize the *laissez-faire* sins of city governments, and at a cost far less than landscape architects' fees? Also, what is the difference between landscape architecture and an earthwork? These are questions awaiting debate in the '80s if this development should continue.

Seattle chose Robert Morris before the others, as a "pilot" artist. His gravel pit is located along a highway that runs through a flat, nondescript stretch of countryside-cum-light industrial sprawl. The site itself is close to and fully visible from the road; a dozen or so random tree stumps, cut to stand three to four feet high, mark the entrance to Morris' esthetic terrain. His handling of the gravel pit is clear and simple, essentially one of grading. He used an ancient form of terracing that follows the natural contours of the slope to hold the soil and prevent slides and erosion.

All the works discussed so far, despite their specific intentions, share certain '70s traits. All (except Sonfist's) are situated in public, though natural places; all seek a rapport with their audience. They expect, however, a private, one-to-one relationship between the individual and the work, regardless of the different levels of awareness which the work can summon in its audience. This art may be open to the public, but it

Alan Sonfist
Time Landscape, A Reconstruction of a Pre-Colonial Forest, 1977

Robert Morris
Untitled, 1979
Kent, Washington
facing east

Lloyd Hamrol
Log Ramps, 1974
Bellingham, Washington
facing west

maintains a low profile, a personal scale. It is not intended to accommodate crowds.

Other artists, moving into the public arena with projects instead of objects, are, however, tackling the question of the public on a larger scale. For them the notion of the audience is collective, not individual. In the past decade, artists, architects, and urban planners have involved themselves in projects of major proportions. Backed by substantial public funds, several extremely successful and highly encouraging results have begun to redraw the boundaries between sculpture, architecture, and urban design. The success of such projects requires collaboration and communication; the failures, as often as not, hang themselves on this issue.[8]

Robert Irwin's piece, presently under construction in Dallas, Texas, combines aspects of both small-scale and large-scale projects. Irwin's installations, whether indoor or outdoor, always draw directly from the site. Often they are about "siting" the viewer, hence their orientation toward the individual. The audience's role in the Dallas piece, however, will be slightly different. The site itself, owned by a commercial developer, borders on an elevated freeway and is divided into three lots by roads, one of which is the freeway access ramp for a main Dallas exit. Thus the audience will, for the most part, see the work from a car, and fairly quickly. Irwin's wall is made of cor-ten steel, quoting a band of the same material along the underside of the elevated road, visible from all parts of the park. The ten-foot-high wall runs straight across the three plots stopping completely at the roads, then disappearing into and emerging from low hills. Where two of the roads intersect, a brick circle will be laid into the pavement,

joining the four sections of street. The brick will be perceived by motorists as a change in surface when they drive over it, heightening attention to the work. Wide openings in the wall at the points where it crosses the brick will allow pedestrians to pass through.

Irwin was originally brought into the project with an NEA Art in Public Places matching grant, but as plans progressed, he became involved with the developer and a landscape architectural firm. Much of the total cost of the project, far exceeding the original grant, is being borne by the developer, who had engaged the landscape firm to work on the park before Irwin was commissioned to do the sculpture.

The archetypal arena for public art has always been the plaza. From the Roman Forum to the *Piazza Navona* to Grand Army Plaza, with General Sherman on his Horse, this public space has epitomized our collective consciousness. Three recent designs, one each by a sculptor, an urban planner, and an architect, demonstrate a renewed concern for an amenity which, historically, has humanized urban life. All, not coincidentally, focus on fountains.

In 1970 Isamu Noguchi was asked, on very short notice, to submit a proposal for a fountain with a $2,000,000 price tag, for the then-unbuilt Hart Plaza in downtown Detroit, Michigan. The site is bounded on one side by the Detroit River, on the other by office buildings and a highway, and is within sight of the

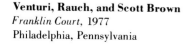

Venturi, Rauch, and Scott Brown
Franklin Court, 1977
Philadelphia, Pennsylvania

Hart Plaza
facing east
(detail of underground skating rink)

Hart Plaza
facing west
(detail of paving and fountain)

Isamu Noguchi
Philip A. Hart Plaza, 1979
Detroit, Michigan
facing south

Lawrence Halprin
Lovejoy Plaza, 1965
(detail of fountain)

Red Grooms
The Bookstore, 1979
Hudson River Museum
Yonkers, New York
(detail of entrance)

See color plate pg. 41

Renaissance Center, a major complex of hotels, apartments, stores, and restaurants that has transformed the inner city. Noguchi came up with a design for the fountain, accompanied by suggestions that would adjust the surroundings to accommodate his idea more favorably than the existing plaza plan. The chairman of the fountain committee happened also to be head of the firm responsible for the plaza. Everyone preferred Noguchi's design and decided to turn the project over to him.

Noguchi then teamed up with the architect Shoji Sadao, and after many versions, arrived at the now completed, two-level plaza with the fountain, an amphitheatre/skating rink, seating, and play areas on top and an underpass, restaurant, and facilities for Detroit's annual Ethnic Festival below. At the main entrance stands an elegant aluminum twisted column. The fountain itself consists of a large ring, twenty-eight feet off the ground, supported by two slanting tubular legs over a shallow, barrel-shaped basin. If it seems to have alighted like some leggy lunar module, that is deliberate. Noguchi explains: "I wanted to make a new fountain, which represents our times and our relationship to outer space."[9] Its appearance is not its only space-age aspect. The water control is totally computerized; some thirty to forty programs continuously adjust the styles of spray from a fine mist ejected from the ring to a huge cylinder of water rising up from the well. Drains at the base of the legs can be closed to flood the surrounding shallow basin for wading.

The plaza has been wildly successful beyond all expectations; so much so, according to Sadao, that the constant mobs of people have generated enormous maintenance problems. But these are being worked out. And it represents, at long last, a large-scale achievement for Noguchi, who has been involved with the design of public spaces since the 1930s. Unfortunately, his ideas were ahead of his time; most were never realized. (Two playgrounds for New York, one for the U.N. and another on Riverside Drive, were squelched by Robert Moses and John Lindsay, supposedly two of the city's more forward-looking public servants.)[10]

Lawrence Halprin's *Lovejoy Plaza* in Portland, Oregon, completed in 1966, brings a completely different sensibility to urban design. An urban planner/architect/ecologist well-known for his interest in the needs of urban dwellers, Halprin was hired by Portland's redevelopment agency to design an interconnected, eight-block stretch of open pedestrian spaces that join downtown Portland with Portland Center, a large-scale project including housing, shops, etc. His

solution encompasses three plazas connected by walkways; *Lovejoy Plaza*, perhaps the most dramatic, adjoins the new housing of Portland Center. Here the plaza has practically *become* the fountain. Water tumbles down a many-layered jumble of roughly cast concrete crags, crevices, and steps that are meant to be played in and climbed on. Halprin makes no secret of the source of their inspiration, describing them as "a man-made evocation of the beauty and excitement of the falling, spurting, flowing, rolling cascades of the High Sierras."[11] Waterfalls, rapids, sprays, and torrents evoke in urban surroundings the romance of the northwest wilderness.

The other focal points of this pedestrian network are intended to complement *Lovejoy Plaza*'s exuberance. Pettigrove Park, a wooded section halfway between *Lovejoy* and downtown, offers a quiet, natural setting and a transition between housing and offices. And downtown, in the forecourt of the Civic Auditorium, is another fountain of quite a different character: a large, sunken, square in the middle of the court is punctuated by multileveled slabs and cubes over which water courses in more regular patterns than *Lovejoy*, like dams. Halprin drew these forms, he says, from the cliffs and mesas of the western landscape. Again, he intends people to enter the fountain.

A third redevelopment project involving a plaza and fountain is currently underway in New Orleans. Though the city is best known for its Creole heritage, it has a substantial Italian population, centered in the section slated for redevelopment. In 1974 the mayor's office held a competition for the design of the *Piazza d'Italia*; a local firm, August Perez and Associates, was chosen. Charles Moore had also submitted a design, with a fountain as the focal point. Perez' design, while it included a fountain, concentrated more on plans for the rest of the plaza. Both drew on Italian architectural themes, and since Perez liked Moore's fountain, the two decided to collaborate.[12] So far, little is finished except Moore's *St. Joseph's Fountain*, since problems arose over the city acting as lessor of the property and a private developer must be found for the rest of the project.

Moore, one of post-modern architecture's wittiest and most distinguished practitioners, has come up with a deliberately eclectic fantasy for the piazza's fountain. It includes a large shallow circular basin surrounded by arcades designed in the five classical orders (A sixth,

"Piazza d'Italia,"
facing east

Charles Moore
"Piazza d'Italia", 1978
New Orleans, Louisiana
evening view facing southwest

See color plate pg. 45

34 dubbed "delicatessen order" by Moore, will serve as the entrance to a restaurant).[13] The water articulates the architectural details, forming leaves, column fluting, etc. At the base of the colonnades, an eighty-foot map of Italy, made of marble, slate, and mirrored tiles, stretches out into the basin. The Arno, the Po, and the Tiber flow down the map, into "seas" surrounding the boot. The arcades, painted in jazzy, post-modern colors, are outlined with neon lights at night. The whole scheme is deliberately historicized, rich, and evocative. "Sited" not only in the plaza itself but in the Italian-American's fantasy of the homeland, it playfully invokes Robert Venturi's theories about the richness of complexity and contradiction, which, not coincidentally, were drawn largely from Italian architecture and cityscapes. Venturi himself has ventured into plaza design, in *Franklin Court* in Philadelphia, for example, where his espousal of the vernacular may be more effective in theory than in practice.

The A.I.A. prize for outlandish public space design really belongs to Red Grooms. Painter, sculptor, architect, urban planner (or *un*planner), and clown, Grooms has brought humor and chaos to the '70s sensibility. His *Ruckus Manhattan* was a Brobdingnagian accumulation of freaked-out skyscrapers and comic-book New Yorkers. His latest caper, *The Bookstore,* is permanently housed at the Hudson River Museum in Yonkers, New York. A *Mad Magazine* version of the Morgan Library combined with a hip rendition of a Lower East Side bookshop, Grooms' work doubles as the museum's shop, selling real catalogues and books alongside the humorous painted titles. And real museum-goers browse alongside shoppers from the artist's cast of goopy characters.

If any overall trend can be detected from the diffuseness of '70s art, it may turn out to be the shift in emphasis from object site. The change is visible in outdoor art, whether individual pieces are truly site-specific or only site-oriented. It has parallels, however, in the work of certain painters, as well as in performance and other impermanent projects. This is an art that presumes the existence of an audience, not one which relies solely on itself. But who is that audience? Is it the general public or does it still consist largely of traditional avant garde? The answer depends, I think, on the degree of nonesthetic content perceivable in any individual work. The notion of land reclamation may make Robert Morris' Seattle work palatable to an ecologically minded art hater. Red Grooms' humor

certainly breaks down any esthetic barriers. Water seems to have a universal appeal. Site-specific work, regardless of its conceptual ambitions, invites the audience in. This in itself is a gesture of public commitment.

But nonesthetic content is not the only answer; for a work to succeed as art it must, of course, have esthetic content as well. The problem the artists must face is how to weld the two. Various possibilities have suggested themselves. Collaborations between disciplines are one possibility; Seattle's enterprise is another. Grooms, Moore, and Oldenburg have all employed humor successfully, though this is tricky to do. Tacha and Fleischner suggest that the small-scale, individually directed project can work as well. It is premature to tell how the change in attitude that evolved during the '70s will resolve itself in the art of the '80s. Boundaries remain tentative; terms have yet to be defined; the problems have by no means been solved. But one thing has become clear: if we are ever again to have a public art, it is the artist, not the public, who will have to make it so.

Nancy Holt
Sun Tunnels, 1976
Great Basin Desert, Utah
(not included in exhibition)

1. Rosalind Krauss, "Sculpture in the Expanded Field," *October*, No. 8, Spring 1979, pp. 31–44.

2. Brian O'Doherty, "Inside The White Cube: Notes on the Gallery Space, Part I," *Artforum*, March 1976, pp. 24–32, " . . . :The Eye and the Spectator, Part II," April 1976, pp. 26–34, " . . . :Context as Content, Part III," November 1976, pp. 38–44.

3. Athena Tacha, *Ten Projects for Staircases*, 1971 (booklet published by the artist).

4. See Athena Tacha, "Rhythm as Form," *Landscape Architecture*, May 1978, pp. 196–205.

5. See Vincent Scully, *The Earth, the Temple and the Gods*, Yale University Press, New Haven and London, 1962.

6. See *The Writings of Robert Smithson*, ed. Nancy Holt, New York: New York University Press, New York, 1979, p. 220.

7. For a more detailed account of the Seattle project, see my "Monument—Sculpture—Earthwork," *Artforum*, October 1979, pp. 32–37.

8. See Jeremy Gilbert–Rolfe, "Capital Follies," *Artforum*, September 1978, pp.66–67, for a discussion of an aborted collaboration between Robert Venturi and Richard Serra for a plaza on Pennsylvania Avenue in Washington, D.C.

9. Exhibition placard, "Isamu Noguchi: The Sculpture of Spaces," Whitney Museum of American Art, February 5–April 6, 1980.

10. Whitney Museum of American Art, *Isamu Noguchi: The Sculpture of Spaces*, 1980, pp. 13, 18.

11. Lawrence Halprin, *Cities*, The M.I.T. Press, Cambridge, Mass., rev. ed. 1972, p. 233.

12. Conversation with R. Allen Eskew of August Perez and Associates.

13. Martin Filler, "The Magic Fountain," *Progressive Architecture*, November 1978, pp. 86–87.

Catalogue of the Exhibition

Information about each site (•) is followed by a list of works in the exhibition. In the site information, dimensions refer to the artwork, or where applicable, are noted as overall site dimensions. Dates indicate the completion of the installation.

All dimensions are in inches unless otherwise indicated. Height precedes width precedes depth. Photographic and documentary material which augmented the exhibition is not included here.

Key: GSA indicates Art in Architecture Program, General Services Administration; NEA indicates Art in Public Places, Visual Arts Program, National Endowment for the Arts

Urban Encounters:
Art Architecture Audience
installation photograph

Stephen Antonakos
Born in St. Nicholas, Gythereion,
Greece, 1926
Lives in New York, New York

• *Incomplete Circles and Squares, Red Neon, 1978,* 1978
Neon
Site: Swimming pool ceiling, 45′ x 75′
Robert Crown Center
Hampshire College
Amherst, Massachusetts
Funding: Hampshire College; NEA

Drawing, 1978
Colored pencil, marker and pen on tissue paper
14 x 21
Lent by the artist

Maquette, 1978
Foamcore, plastic coated copper wire
2½ x 15¾ x 30
Lent by the artist

Jennifer Bartlett
Born in Long Beach, California, 1941
Lives in New York, New York

• *Swimmers Atlanta,* 1979
Enamel on steel, oil on canvas
Site: Lobby, 20′ x 160′ x 22′
Richard B. Russell Federal Building
and U.S. Courthouse
75 Spring Street, S. W.
Atlanta, Georgia
Funding: GSA

Study for *Swimmers Atlanta,* 1979
Colored pencil, pencil on graph paper
17 x 66
Lent by the artist

Study for *Swimmers Atlanta:*
Boat, 1979
Colored pencil, pencil on graph paper
20¼ x 22⅜
Lent by the artist

Study for *Swimmers Atlanta:*
Bottle, 1979
Colored pencil, pencil on graph paper
17¾ x 22⅜
Lent by the artist

Study for *Swimmers Atlanta:*
Buoy, 1979
Colored pencil, pencil on graph paper
17¾ x 22⅜
Lent by the artist

Study for *Swimmers Atlanta: Eel,* 1979
Colored pencil, pencil on graph paper
17¾ x 22⅜
Lent by the artist

Study for *Swimmers Atlanta:*
Flare, 1979
Colored pencil, pencil on graph paper
17¾ x 22⅜
Lent by the artist

Study for *Swimmers Atlanta: Iceberg*
(White), 1979
Colored pencil, pencil on graph paper
17¾ x 22⅜
Lent by the artist

Study for *Swimmers Atlanta:*
Rock, 1979
Colored pencil, pencil on graph paper
17¾ x 22⅜
Lent by the artist

Study for *Swimmers Atlanta:*
Seaweed, 1979
Colored pencil, pencil on graph paper
17¾ x 22⅜
Lent by the artist

Study for *Swimmers Atlanta: Whirlpool*
(Black), 1979
Colored pencil, pencil on graph paper
17¾ x 22⅜
Lent by the artist

Urban Encounters:
Art Architecture Audience
installation photograph

Alexander Calder
Born in Philadelphia,
Pennsylvania, 1898
Died in New York, New York, 1976

• *"La Grande Vitesse,"* 1969
Painted steel plate
43' x 30' x 54'
City plaza
Vandenberg Plaza
Ottawa and Michigan Avenues
Grand Rapids, Michigan
Funding: City of Grand Rapids; community contributions; Grand Rapids Foundation; Keeler Foundation; Lindbert; NEA; Old Kent Bank; Seidman; Steelcase; Union Bank; Wege Foundation; Women's Committee of Grand Rapids Art Museum

Happy Valentine, 1970
Gouache on paper
23¼ x 31
Lent by Mr. and Mrs. M.S. Keeler II

Maquette, 1968
Painted steel
18½ x 24 x 10½
Lent by the National Endowment for the Arts, Washington, D.C.

Mark di Suvero
Born in Shanghai, China, 1933
Lives in Petaluma, California

• *Under Sky/One Family,* 1979
Cor-ten steel
54' x 40' x 90'
Riverfront
East Pratt Street
Inner Harbor, Baltimore, Maryland
Funding: City of Baltimore; NEA

After completion drawing, 1979
Felt tip pen on paper
17 x 14
Lent by the artist, courtesy R. Bellamy

Maquette, 1977
Cor-ten steel
9¼ x 19¼ x 17¼
Lent by City of Baltimore, William Donald Schaefer, Mayor; courtesy the Department of Housing and Community Development

Original submission drawing, 1977
Felt tip pen, ink on paper
18½ x 23½
Lent by the artist, courtesy
R. Bellamy

Original submission drawing, 1977
Felt tip pen, ink on paper
18½ x 23½
Lent by the artist, courtesy
R. Bellamy

Original submission drawing, 1977
Felt tip pen, ink on paper
18 x 22½
Lent by the artist, courtesy
R. Bellamy

Original submission drawing, 1977
Felt tip pen, ink on paper
18½ x 22½
Lent by the artist, courtesy
R. Bellamy

Rafael Ferrer
Born in Santurce, Puerto Rico, 1933
Lives in Philadelphia, Pennsylvania

• *Puerto Rican Sun,* 1979
Cor-ten steel, enamel paint
25' x 25' x 1'
City lot
Community Garden Park
156th and Fox Streets
Bronx, New York
Funding: Brown Council on the Arts; Citibank; Con Edison; community contributions; NEA; New York City Department of Parks and Recreation; New York State Council on the Arts

Drawing, 1979
Watercolor on handmade paper
13½ x 12¾
Lent by the artist, courtesy Hamilton Gallery of Contemporary Art

Drawing, 1979
Watercolor on handmade paper
15½ x 12
Lent by the artist, courtesy Hamilton Gallery of Contemporary Art

Drawing, 1979
Pastel on paper
14 x 16¾
Lent by the artist, courtesy Hamilton Gallery of Contemporary Art

Engineer's drawing, 1979
Diazo print
24 x 36
Lent by Nicole Levin

Maquette, 1979
Cor-ten steel, enamel paint
36 x 43 x 12½
Lent by the artist, courtesy Hamilton Gallery of Contemporary Art

Stephen Antonakos
Incomplete Circles and Squares,
Red Neon, 1978, 1978
Amherst, Massachusetts

Richard Fleischner
Born in New York, New York, 1944
Lives in Providence, Rhode Island

• *Cow Island Project*, 1978
Existing landscape elements, granite
Site: City park, 2-acre island
Cow Island, Roger Williams Park
9th and Elmwood Avenue
Providence, Rhode Island
Funding: Community contributions;
Department of Public Parks, City of
Providence; NEA; U.S. Department of
Commerce; U.S. Department of
Interior

Drawing, 1977
Pencil on tracing paper
$42\,^5/_{16}$ x $31\,^5/_8$
Lent by the artist

Site plan, 1977
Ink and pencil on paper
$23\,^7/_{16}$ x $25\,^5/_8$
Lent by the artist

Red Grooms
Born in Nashville, Tennessee, 1937
Lives in New York, New York

• *The Bookstore*, 1979
Mixed media
Site: Museum shop, 25' x 20' x 11'
Hudson River Museum
511 Warburton Avenue
Yonkers, New York
Funding: William Randolph Hearst
Foundation; IBM Corporation; NEA;
Sarah I. Schieffelin Residuary Trust;
Wells, Rich, Greene, Inc.

Maquette, 1978
Foamcore, paper, watercolor
25 x 26 x 30½
Lent by the artist

Working drawings, 1978
Felt tip pen on paper
10 drawings, each 14 x 11
4 double-sheet drawings, each 22 x 14
Lent by the artist

Lawrence Halprin
Born in New York, New York, 1916
Lives in San Francisco, California

• *Lovejoy Plaza*, 1965
Poured-in-place concrete, water
Site: Pedestrian mall; fountain,
60' x 60'; plaza, 200' x 200'
One block north of Lincoln Street and
4th Avenue
Portland, Oregon
Funding: Redevelopment Agency
of Portland

Basic layout plan, c. 1963–64
Colored pencil, pencil on tracing paper
36 x 46 ·
Lent by Lawrence Halprin,
Lawrence Halprin and Associates

Layout, grading plan and details,
c. 1963–64
Photostat
36 x 46
Lent by Lawrence Halprin
Lawrence Halprin and Associates

Overall design of Portland Open Space
Sequence, c. 1963–64
Colored pencil, pencil on paper
35 x 46
Lent by Lawrence Halprin,
Lawrence Halprin and Associates

Sketches for *Lovejoy Plaza*,
hand-colored, 1980
Colored pencil, xerox on paper
Four drawings, each 10½ x 8
Lent by Lawrence Halprin,
Lawrence Halprin and Associates

Structural details, c. 1963–64
Colored pencil, pencil on paper
36 x 46
Lent by Lawrence Halprin,
Lawrence Halprin and Associates

Urban Encounters:
Art Architecture Audience
installation photograph

Lloyd Hamrol
Born in San Francisco, California, 1937
Lives in Venice, California

• *Log Ramps,* 1974
Cedar logs, steel cable
9' x 36' x 36'
Campus
Western Washington State University
Near Arntzen Hall and Environmental Studies Center
Bellingham, Washington
Funding: Art Department, Bureau for Faculty Research, and Environmental Studies Center of Western Washington State University; NEA

Log Ramps, 1975
Black and white videotape
7½ minutes, sound
Lent by the artist

Notes on Log Ramps, 1974–80
Ink, pencil on board
23 x 29
Lent by the artist

Michael Heizer
Born in Berkeley, California, 1944
Lives in New York, New York

• *Adjacent Against Upon,* 1976
Concrete, granite
9' x 130' x 25'
City park
Myrtle Edwards Park
Alaskan Way between West Bay and West Thomas
Seattle, Washington
Funding: NEA; Seattle Arts Commission

Drawings for Seattle Project, 1975
Ball point pen on graph paper
Four drawings, each 17 x 22
Lent by Charles Cowles

Maquette, 1977–78
Wood
1⅞ x 36 x 11
Lent anonymously

Robert Indiana
Born in New Castle, Indiana, 1928
Lives in Vinalhaven, Maine

• *MECCA,* 1977
Enamel paint on wood floor
Site: Basketball court, 100' x 56'
Milwaukee Exposition Convention Center Arena (MECCA)
500 West Kilbourne Avenue
Milwaukee, Wisconsin
Funding: MECCA

Study for *MECCA,* 1977
Collage
36 x 48
Lent by MECCA

Study for *MECCA,* 1977
Collage
36 x 48
Lent by MECCA

Study for *MECCA,* 1977
Collage
36 x 48
Lent by MECCA

Study for *MECCA,* 1977
Collage
36 x 48
Lent by MECCA

Robert Irwin
Born in Long Beach, California, 1928
Lives in Los Angeles, California

• *Untitled,* expected completion, Spring, 1981
Cor-ten steel
10' x 700' x 1'
City park
Carpenter Plaza, Dallas
East Portal Park
Dallas, Texas
Funding: City of Dallas; NEA; Southland Foundation

Architectural rendering, 1979
Photostat
24 x 42
Lent by the artist

Architectural rendering, 1979
Pencil on paper
24 x 93
Lent by the artist

Demonstration model, 1980
Clay, steel
Dimensions variable
Reconstructed for the exhibition following the directions of the artist

Charles Moore
Born in Benton Harbor, Michigan, 1925
Lives in Los Angeles, California

• *"Piazza d'Italia,"* 1978
Exterior plaster, granite, marble, neon, slate, stainless steel, steel framing
Site: Fountain and plaza, 100' radius
Between Poydras and Lafayette Streets
New Orleans, Louisiana
Funding: Economic Development Administration of the City of New Orleans

Architectural drawing, 1976
Ink and pencil on tracing paper
22 x 31
Lent by Charles Moore, Urban Innovations Group, Los Angeles

Architectural drawing, 1976
Ink and pencil on tracing paper
23¾ x 25¾
Lent by Charles Moore, Urban Innovations Group, Los Angeles

Design sketches, 1976
Pencil on tracing paper
Two drawings, each 12 x 20
Lent by Charles Moore, Urban Innovations Group, Los Angeles

Robert Morris
Born in Kansas City, Missouri, 1931
Lives in Gardiner, New York

• *Untitled,* 1979
Earth, grass, trees
Site: Reclaimed land, 1800' x 600'
40th Place South at South 216th Street
Kent, Washington
Funding: Federal Bureau of Mines; King County Arts Commission; NEA

Maquette, 1979
Acrylic, foamcore
7½ x 39 x 18
Lent by the King County Arts Commission

Proposed Grading and Utilities, 1979
Diazo print
31 x 49
Lent by the King County Arts Commission

Temporary Erosion Control, 1979
Diazo print
30¼ x 48¼
Lent by the King County Arts Commission

Louise Nevelson
Born in Kiev, Russia, 1900
Lives in New York, New York

• *Shadows and Flags,* 1978
Cor-ten steel
Site: City park, 82' x 188' x 200'
Louise Nevelson Park
Liberty Street, Maiden Lane, and Williams Street
New York, New York
Funding: Mildred Andrews Fund; Office of Development of the City of New York; community corporate sponsors

Partial Model for *Shadows and Flags, Column,* 1977–79
Welded steel
36⅛ x 15¼ x 12
Lent by The Pace Gallery

Isamu Noguchi
Born in Los Angeles, California, 1904
Lives in Long Island City, New York

• *Philip A. Hart Plaza,* 1979
Concrete, glass, granite, metal, translucent acrylic, wood
Site: City plaza, 680' x 710'
Jefferson and Auditorium Drive
Detroit, Michigan
Funding: Capital Gifts Committee of the City of Detroit; Anne Thompson Dodge; D. M. Ferry, Jr. Trustee Company

Maquette: *The Horace E. Dodge and Son Memorial Fountain at Hart Plaza, Detroit,* 1972–78
Wood
17 x 6' x 6'
Lent by the artist

Plaza site plan, n.d.
Blueprint
30½ x 42
Lent by Noguchi Fountains, Inc.

Sub-plaza site plan, n.d.
Blueprint
30½ x 42
Lent by Noguchi Fountains, Inc.

Jennifer Bartlett
Swimmers Atlanta: Buoys, 1979
Atlanta, Georgia
(detail, central panel)

TP 2/2   31 IX '77   R Indiana

Robert Indiana
Study for *MECCA,* 1977
collage, 36″ x 48″

Red Grooms
The Bookstore, 1979
Hudson River Museum
Yonkers, New York
(detail of interior)

Urban Encounters:
Art Architecture Audience
installation photograph

Claes Oldenburg
Born in Stockholm, Sweden, 1929
Lives in New York, New York

• *Clothespin*, 1976
Cor-ten steel, stainless steel
45' x 12'3¼" x 53'¾"
City plaza
Centre Square
1500 Market Street
Philadelphia, Pennsylvania
Funding: Centre Square Developers

Clothespin elevations, 1973–74
Pencil on paper
56½ x 32½
Lent by the artist

Engineer's drawing of *Clothespin*,
1975–79
Pencil on paper
56½ x 42
Lent by J. Robert Jennings

Engineer's drawing of pedestal base,
1975–79
Pencil on paper
24 x 36¼
Lent by J. Robert Jennings

Maquette, 1976–79
Cor-ten steel, stainless steel
60 x 22¾ x 19¾
Lent by the artist

Eero Saarinen
Born in Kirkkonummi, Finland, 1910
Died in Ann Arbor, Michigan, 1961

• *Jefferson National Expansion
Memorial*, 1965
Concrete, stainless steel
630' x 630' x 18'
National park
Jefferson National Expansion Memorial
Park
11 North 4th Street
St. Louis, Missouri
Funding: City of St. Louis; Jefferson
National Expansion Memorial
Association; National Parks Service;
United States Territorial Expansion
Memorial Commission

Maquette, n.d.
Acrylic paint, plastic, wood
19 x 85 x 49
Lent by Jefferson National Expansion
Memorial Association

Memorial to the Dream, 1963
Film
27 minutes, color
Producer: Charles Guggenheim
Lent by Jefferson National Expansion
Memorial Association

Joel Meyerowitz
The Arch, 1978
Four photographs, each 7½ x 9½
Lent by the artist, courtesy Witkin
Gallery

Alan Sonfist
Born in New York, New York, 1946
Lives in New York, New York

• *Time Landscape, A Reconstruction of a
Pre-Colonial Forest*, 1977
Plants indigenous to site
Site: City park, presently 9,000 square
feet on an 18,000 square foot lot
La Guardia Place between Houston and
Bleeker Streets
New York, New York
Funding: Chase Manhattan Foundation
for Environmental and Fine Arts;
Citibank Foundation; community
contributions; Con Edison Foundation;
Charles Gilman Foundation; National
Shopping Centers, Inc.; NEA

*Aerial View of Time Landscape, A
Reconstruction of a Pre-Colonial
Forest*, 1969–78
Blueprint
21 x 37
Lent anonymously

Aerial View of Time Landscape, A Reconstruction of a Pre-Colonial Forest—Vegetation Locations, 1969–78
Blueprint
20 x 60
Lent anonymously

Cross-sectional View of Time Landscape, A Reconstruction of a Pre-Colonial Forest, 1969–78
Blueprint
21 x 37
Lent anonymously

Drawing of Time Landscape, A Reconstruction of a Pre-Colonial Forest, 1965
Ink on paper
22 x 30
Lent anonymously

Model of the Hemlock Forest, Low Open Area, 1965
Earth, red maple, wild cherry
13 x 13
Lent anonymously

Model of the Hemlock Forest, Lower Area, 1965
Beech, earth, hemlock
15 x 15
Lent anonymously

Model of the Hemlock Forest, Open Area, 1965
Earth, grey birch, red cedar
14 x 15
Lent anonymously

Model of the Hemlock Forest, Upper Hills, 1965
Earth, red and white oaks
16 x 12
Lent anonymously

George Sugarman
Born in New York, New York, 1912
Lives in New York, New York

• *Baltimore Federal,* 1978
Painted aluminum
19' x 45' x 45'
City plaza
Edward A. Garmatz Federal Building
and U.S. Courthouse
101 West Lombard Street
Baltimore, Maryland
Funding: GSA

Study for Sculpture in Relation to Architecture, 1979
Maquette for an unrealized project
Composition board, painted aluminum
31¾ x 60 x 48
Lent by Robert Miller Gallery

Untitled, 1979–80
Color videotape
10 minutes, sound
Lent by the artist

Athena Tacha
Born in Larissa, Greece, 1936
Lives in New York, New York

• *Streams,* 1976
Cement block, concrete, pebbles, pink pumice, yellow sandstone
10' x 20' x 30'
City park
Vine Street Park by Plum Creek
Oberlin, Ohio
Funding: City of Oberlin; community contributions; NEA; Ohio Arts Council

First Drawing for Streams, 1975
Felt tip pen on graph paper
11 x 17
Lent by the artist

Ground Plan for Streams, 1975
Felt tip pen on vellum
30 x 36
Lent by the artist

Maquette, 1975–76
Corrugated board, glue, paint, plexiglass, pumice stone, sawdust, steel wool, vermiculite
11 x 36 x 30
Lent by the artist

Three Foundation Terraces With Expansion Joints, 1976
Felt tip pen on graph paper
17¼ x 22
Lent by the artist

Rafael Ferrer
Puerto Rican Sun, 1979
Bronx, New York
facing southeast and northwest

Charles Moore
"Piazza d'Italia," 1978
New Orleans, Louisiana
facing east (detail)

George Sugarman
Baltimore Federal, 1978
Baltimore, Maryland
facing southeast

This list is intended to indicate the diversity and geographical distribution of public art created by painters and sculptors during the past fifteen years. In the context of this exhibition, works on museum grounds are generally not considered public art.

Dimensions refer to the artwork or, where applicable, are noted as overall site dimensions. Height precedes width precedes depth. Dates indicate the completion of the installation. The sites are cross-referenced by geographical location on page 57.

Compiling this list proved to be difficult, not only in determining the selections, but in acquiring what was felt to be useful information (exact street addresses or sponsors, for example). Though everyone contacted was sincerely interested in being helpful, diverse professions differ in the kinds of information that they preserve. Therefore, a few of the listings may be incomplete. It is hoped, however, that the format that has been devised will be useful in future endeavors.

Carl Andre
Stone Field Sculpture, 1977
Hartford, Connecticut

Carl Andre
Stone Field Sculpture, 1977
36 uncut glacial boulders
Site dimensions: 53' x 290'
Hartford Public Green
Main and Gold Streets
Hartford, Connecticut
Funding: Hartford Foundation for Public Giving; NEA

Stephen Antonakos
Red Neon Circle Fragments on a Blue Wall, 1978
Neon tubes on enameled panels
10' x 68'
Facade of Federal Building and U.S. Courthouse
41 North Perry Street Dayton, Ohio
Funding: GSA

Four Walls for Atlanta, 1980
Acrylic paint and neon
Site dimensions: Four stepped ceilings, each 15' x 30'
Escalator well, Landside Air Terminal
Atlanta Airport
Atlanta, Georgia
Funding: Atlanta Airline Construction Funds; contracting airlines; Federal Department of Transportation; NEA

Richard Anuszkiewicz
Untitled, 1972
Bulletin paint, outdoor enamel
115' x 52'
Exterior of Young Women's Christian Association
50th Street and 8th Avenue
New York, New York
Funding: City Walls, Inc.; NEA

Judith F. Baca
Great Wall of Los Angeles,
1976 - present
Specially developed mural paint
13' x 1700' long (dimensions to date)
Culvert along Coldwater Canyon between Oxnard and Burbank Boulevards
Studio City, San Fernando Valley, California
Funding: Army Corp of Engineers; City of Los Angeles, Department of Cultural Affairs, Summer Youth Program; Juvenile Justice System, San Fernando Valley

Leonard Baskin
The Three Presidents from Tennessee, 1976
Bronze
Three panels, each 2' x 1'4" x 4"
Lobby of Federal Building and U.S. Courthouse
801 Broadway Street
Nashville, Tennessee
Funding: GSA

Jack Beal
The History of Labor in America, 1977
Oil on canvas
Four panels, each 12' x 12'6"
Lobby of Department of Labor Building
200 Constitution Avenue, N.W.
Washington, D.C.
Funding: GSA

Lynda Benglis
Patang, 1980
Satin appliqu
Two panels, each 15' x 40'
Eastern Airlines Ticket Area
Landside Air Terminal
Atlanta Airport
Atlanta, Georgia
Funding: Atlanta Airline Construction Funds; contracting airlines; Federal Department of Transportation; NEA

Ronald Bladen
Cosmic Seed, 1980
Painted steel, stainless steel
23' x 20' x 4'
Grounds of Iowa State Capitol
East 12th and Grand Streets
Des Moines, Iowa
Funding: NEA; State of Iowa

Ilya Bolotowsky
Chicago Murals, 1976
Porcelain enamel on steel
14' x 45'
Lobby of Great Lakes Program Center
600 West Madison Street
Chicago, Illinois
Funding: GSA

Louise Bourgeois
Untitled, 1978
Concrete, marble, steel coated
with epoxy
3' x 10' x 10'
Plaza of Norris Cotton Federal Building
275 Chestnut Street
Manchester, New Hampshire
Funding: GSA

Bill Brand
Masstransiscope, 1980
Fluorescent lamps, ink,
retroflective sheeting
300' x 12'
Myrtle Avenue Subway Station
Brooklyn, New York
Funding: American Stock Exchange;
Chase Manhattan Bank; Con Edison;
Merrill, Lynch, Pierce, Fenner &
Smith, Inc.; NEA; New York State
Council on the Arts

Alexander Calder
Flamingo, 1974
Painted steel plate
53' x 24' x 60'
Federal Center Plaza
230 South Dearborn Street
Chicago, Illinois
Funding: GSA

Four Arches, 1974
Steel painted red
45' x 63' x 63'
Plaza of Security Pacific National
Bank Building
333 South Hope Street
Los Angeles, California
Funding: The Community
Redevelopment Agency

Jack Beal
The History of Labor in America, 1977
Washington, D.C.

Ilya Bolotowsky
Chicago Murals, 1976
Chicago, Illinois

Lynda Benglis
Patang, 1980
Atlanta, Georgia

Mark di Suvero
Victor's Lament, 1979
Allentown, Pennsylvania

Jackie Ferrara
Untitled, 1980
Carbondale, Illinois

Jose de Rivera
Construction #150, 1974
Stainless steel
3'9" x 5' x 3'2"
Washington Square Mall
109 West Michigan Avenue
Lansing, Michigan
Funding: City of Lansing; NEA

Mark di Suvero
Motu, 1977
Cor-ten steel, rubber
35' x 38' x 54'
Plaza of Gerald R. Ford Federal
Building and U.S. Courthouse
110 Michigan Avenue, N.W.
Grand Rapids, Michigan
Funding: GSA

Victor's Lament, 1979
Cor-ten steel
28' x 32'6" x 32'6"
Campus of Muhlenberg College
Chew Street
Allentown, Pennsylvania
Funding: Philip and Muriel Berman;
NEA

Jean Dubuffet
Group of Four Trees, 1972
Aluminum, concrete, epoxy painted
with polyurethane, fiberglass, steel
42' x 32' x 32'
Chase Manhattan Plaza
William and Pine Streets
New York, New York
Funding: David Rockefeller

Dale Eldred
Untitled, 1973
Sand, steel
42' x 15' x 15'
Campus of Grand Valley State College
Lake Michigan Drive
Grand Rapids, Michigan
Funding: Private donor

Jackie Ferrara
Untitled, 1980
Cedar
15'6" x 24' x 14'
Grounds of Federal Building
250 West Cherry Street
Carbondale, Illinois
Funding: GSA

Richard Fleischner
Chain Link Maze, 1978
Chain link fence
8' x 61' x 61'
Campus of University of
Massachusetts/Amherst
Stadium Drive
Amherst, Massachusetts
Funding: NEA; University of
Massachusetts

Sod Maze, 1974
Sod-covered earth
1'6" x 150' x 150'
Grounds of Chateau-sur-mer
Bellevue Avenue
Newport, Rhode Island
Funding: Anonymous donors; NEA

Untitled, 1980
Granite and unfinished cor-ten steel
Site dimensions: 300' x 300' x 40'
Grounds of Social Security
Administration Center
6401 Security Boulevard
Woodlawn, Maryland
Funding: GSA

Sam Gilliam
Triple Variant/Atlanta, 1979
Acrylic, aluminum beam,
fabric, marble, oil
15' x 42' x 4'
Lobby of Richard B. Russell Federal
Building
75 Spring Street, S. W.
Atlanta, Georgia
Funding: GSA

Richard Fleischner
Sod Maze, 1974
Newport, Rhode Island

Nancy Holt
Rock Rings, 1978
Bellingham, Washington

Charles Ginnever
Protagoras, 1976
Cor-ten steel
10′ x 30′ x 14′
Grounds of Federal Building
and U.S. Courthouse
316 North Robert Street
St. Paul, Minnesota
Funding: GSA

Red Grooms
Way Down East, 1979
Iron enamel on aluminum
8′ x 18′ x 12′
Campus of Northern Kentucky
State University
Nunn Drive
Highland Heights, Kentucky
Funding: NEA; Northern Kentucky
State University

Richard Haas
Untitled, 1975
Outdoor enamel paint
60′ x 70′
Exterior of private cooperative
loft building
Greene and Prince Streets
New York, New York
Funding: City Walls, Inc.

Dimitri Hadzi
River Legend, 1976
Basalt
10′ x 13′ x 3′
Plaza of Federal Building
1220 3rd Avenue, S.W.
Portland, Oregon
Funding: GSA

Lloyd Hamrol
Redoubling Wallpath, 1977
Cement, sandbags, soil
5′4″ x 4′6″ x 70′
Campus of California State
University at Fullerton
College Drive
Fullerton, California
Funding: Community contributions;
NEA

Thronapolis, 1979
Redwood
6′6″ x 26′ x 20′
Lower plaza of Richard B. Russell
Federal Building
75 Spring Street, S.W.
Atlanta, Georgia
Funding: GSA

Duane Hatchett
Equilateral Six, 1975
Painted aluminum
12′6″ x 8′ x 14′
Grounds of Federal Building
and U.S. Courthouse
100 State Street
Rochester, New York
Funding: GSA

Al Held
Order/Disorder/Ascension/Descension, 1977
Acrylic on canvas
Two panels, each 13′ x 90′
Lobby of Social Security
Administration Mid-Atlantic Program
Center
300 Spring Garden Street
Philadelphia, Pennsylvania
Funding: GSA

Douglas Hollis
The Wind Organ, 1980
Aluminum piping
Site dimensions: 40′ x 20′
Dam Site 16 on Papio Project
Standing Bear Lake
Omaha, Nebraska
Funding: Metro Arts; NEA; Nebraska
Arts Council; private donations

Nancy Holt
Rock Rings, 1978
Brown Mountain stone schist from
British Columbia
10′ x 40′ x 40′
South campus area of Western
Washington University
Bellingham, Washington
Funding: Artist's contribution; NEA;
Virginia Wright Fund; Washington
State Arts Commission; Western
Washington University Art Fund

Richard Hunt
Richmond Cycle, 1976
Bronze plate
10′10″ x 54′4″ x 8′9″
Plaza of Social Security Administration
Western Program Center
1221 Nevin Avenue
Richmond, California
Funding:GSA

Robert Indiana
Love, 1976
Painted steel
6′ x 6′ x 3′
John F. Kennedy Plaza
16th and John F. Kennedy Boulevard
Philadelphia, Pennsylvania
Funding: F. Eugene Dixon

Al Held
Order/Disorder/Ascension/Descension, 1977
Philadelphia, Pennsylvania

Douglas Hollis
The Wind Organ, 1980
Omaha, Nebraska

Robert Irwin
Untitled (Filigreed Steel Line for Wellesley College), 1980
Stainless steel
2′2″ x 120′ x ⅜″
Campus of Wellesley College
Between Lake Waban and Margaret Clapp Library
Wellesley, Massachusetts
Funding: George and Lois Pattison de Menil; Mildred Cooper Glimcher; NEA; Susan Marley Newhouse; Mabel Louise Riley Charitable Trust; William Underwood Co.

Valerie Jaudon
Untitled, 1977
Oil-based latex paint
7′6″ x 22′
Lobby of Insurance Company of North America
17th and Arch Streets
Philadelphia, Pennsylvania
Funding: Insurance Company of North America

Donald Judd
Box, 1975
Aluminum plate
12′ x 8′ x 8′
Campus of Northern Kentucky State University
Nunn Drive
Highland Heights, Kentucky
Funding: NEA; State of Kentucky

Alex Katz
Five Women, New York Times Square Mural, 1977
Sign paint on aluminum panels
7′4″ x 20′6″
Billboard on Times Square
7th Avenue and 42nd Street
New York, New York
Funding: City Walls Project of the New York State Agency for the Arts

William King
Caritas, 1978
Aluminum
22′ x 32′ x 6′
Plaza of Federal Building and U.S. Courthouse
2 South Main Street
Akron, Ohio
Funding: GSA

Joseph E. Kinnebrew
Fish Ladder, 1975
Aggregate concrete
38′ x 34′ x 65′
Riverbank at 600 Front Street, N.W.
Grand Rapids, Michigan
Funding: City of Grand Rapids; NEA

Lyman Kipp
Highline, 1976
Painted steel
18′ x 5′ x 7′
Plaza of Federal Building
6230 Van Nuys Boulevard
Van Nuys, California
Funding: GSA

Gerhardt Knodel
Sky Ribbons: An Oklahoma Tribute, 1978
Natural and synthetic fibers
11′7″ x 14′7″ x 8′2″
Mezzanine of Alfred P. Murray Federal Building
200 5th Street, N.W.
Oklahoma City, Oklahoma
Funding: GSA

Rockne Krebs
White Light, White Rainbow, White Twister, White Tornado, 1979
Aluminum tubes, glass prisms, neon tubes
40′ x 53′ x 53′
Atrium of Federal Building
444 S.E. Quincy Street
Topeka, Kansas
Funding: GSA

Sol LeWitt
One, Two, Three, 1979
Painted aluminum
14′9″ x 14′9″ x 29′
Plaza of Federal Building
Clinton and Water Streets
Syracuse, New York
Funding: GSA

Robert Irwin
Untitled, 1980
Wellesley, Massachusetts

Sol LeWitt
One, Two, Three, 1979
Syracuse, New York

Alexander Liberman
Covenant, 1975
Rolled sheets of milled steel
45′ x 50′ x 22′
Campus of University of Pennsylvania
39th Street and Locust Walk
Philadelphia, Pennsylvania
Funding: NEA; One Percent
Fine Arts Fund

Roy Lichtenstein
Mermaid, 1979
Concrete, steel, water
21′ x 24′ x 11′
Grounds of the Theater of the
Performing Arts
17th Street and Washington Avenue
Miami Beach, Florida
Funding: Community contributions;
NEA

Robert Richard Maki
Trapezoid E, 1975
Aluminum
12′ x 15′ x 10′
Plaza of Federal Building and U.S.
Courthouse
211 East 7th Avenue
Eugene, Oregon
Funding: GSA

Robert Mangold
*Correlation: Two White Line Diagonals
and Two Arcs With a Sixteen-Foot
Radius*, 1978
Porcelain enamel on steel
Two panels: 16′ x 16′, 8′ x 8′
Facade of Federal Building and U.S.
Courthouse
85 Marconi Boulevard
Columbus, Ohio
Funding: GSA

Ed McGowin
Mississippi Inscape, 1979
Clay tablets, found objects,
precast concrete
26′ x 21′6″ x 4′7″
Plaza of Federal Building
100 West Capitol Street
Jackson, Mississippi
Funding: GSA

Clement Meadmore
Out of There, 1976
Painted steel
6′3″ x 16′7″ x 8′9″
Plaza of Hale Boggs Federal
Building and U.S. Courthouse
500 Camp Street
New Orleans, Louisiana
Funding: GSA

Henry Moore
Reclining Figure, 1965
Bronze
16′ x 30′ x 30′
Reflecting pool at Lincoln Center
Broadway between 62nd
and 65th Streets
New York, New York
Funding: Albert A. List Foundation

Robert Morris
Untitled (Steam Sculpture), 1974
Rocks, steam
12′ x 12′
Campus of Western Washington
University
Bellingham, Washington
Funding: Art allowance from central
cooling plant construction funds

X, 1974
Asphalt, earth
Site dimensions: 280′ x 550′
Grounds overlooking Belknap Park
30 Coldbrook Street
Grand Rapids, Michigan
Funding: City of Grand Rapids;
Michigan Council for the Arts; NEA;
Women's Committee of the Grand
Rapids Art Museum

Robert Murray
Quinnipiac, 1975
Aluminum, cor-ten steel
18′ x 17′6″ x 14′
Plaza of Fine Arts Center
University of Massachusetts
Amherst, Massachusetts
Funding: NEA; University Alumni
Fund

Max Neuhaus
*Underground Music,
Times Square*, 1977
Electronic cord, speaker, subway grille
set in concrete
Dimensions variable
Beneath the street at Broadway
between 45th and 46th Streets
at 7th Avenue
New York, New York
Funding: NEA; New York Telephone;
New York Transit Authority; private
donors; Rockefeller Foundation

Louise Nevelson
Bicentennial Dawn, 1976
White painted wood
15′ x 90′ x 30′
Lobby of James A. Byrne U.S.
Courthouse
601 Market Street
Philadelphia, Pennsylvania
Funding: GSA

Sky Tree, 1976
Black cor-ten steel
54′ x 12′ x 14′
Plaza of Embarcadero Center
Three Embarcadero Center
Front Street between Sacramento
and Clay Streets
San Francisco, California
Funding: John Portman; San Francisco
Redevelopment Authority; Prudential
Life Insurance Company of America

Louise Nevelson
Bicentennial Dawn, 1976
Philadelphia, Pennsylvania

Robert Morris
Untitled (Steam Sculpture), 1974
Bellingham, Washington

Claes Oldenburg
Crusoe's Umbrella, 1979
Des Moines, Iowa

Beverly Pepper
Amphisculpture, 1975
Bedminster, New Jersey

Barnett Newman
Broken Obelisk —Dedicated to Dr. Martin Luther King, 1971
Cor-ten steel
26′ x 10′6″ x 10′6″
Rothko Chapel
3900 Yupon Street
Houston, Texas
Funding: The Menil Foundation

Isamu Noguchi
Rhombohedron, 1967
Painted aluminum on steel frame
28′ x 16′ x 16′
Marine Midland Plaza
140 Broadway
New York, New York
Funding: Marine Midland Bank

Sky-Viewing Sculpture, 1969
Brick pedestals, stainless steel
pins, welded steel
10′ x 10′ x 10′
Red Square at Western Washington University
Bellingham, Washington
Funding: Art allowance from Miller Hall Construction Fund

Claes Oldenburg
Batcolumn, 1977
Painted steel
101′ x 9′9″ x 9′9″
Plaza of Great Lakes Program Center
600 West Madison Street
Chicago, Illinois
Funding: GSA

Crusoe's Umbrella, 1979
Painted steel
33′ x 37′ x 57′
Nollen's Plaza, Des Moines
Civic Center
3rd and Locust Streets
Des Moines, Iowa
Funding: Mr. and Mrs. Sigurd Anderson; The Bankers' Life of Des Moines; The Gardiner and Florence Call Cowles Foundation; Mr. and Mrs. Ralph Green; The Richard Levitt Family; Mrs. E. T. Meredith; NEA

Beverly Pepper
Amphisculpture, 1975
Concrete, earth
8′ x 200′ x 14′
Grounds of AT & T Headquarters
Route 202/206 North
Bedminster, New Jersey
Funding: AT & T

Phaedrus, 1978
Steel plates
19′ x 8′ x 19′
Plaza of Federal Reserve Bank
100 North 6th Street
Philadelphia, Pennsylvania
Funding: Federal Reserve Bank

Pablo Picasso
Untitled, 1967
Cor-ten steel
50′ x 20′ x 30′
Richard J. Daley Plaza
66 West Washington Plaza
Chicago, Illinois
Funding: Gift of the artist; private foundations

Arnaldo Pomodoro
Grande Disco, 1974
Polished bronze
15′ x 15′ x 1′6″
Plaza of North Carolina National Bank
One North Carolina National Bank
Trade and Tryon Streets
Charlotte, North Carolina
Funding: Carter & Associates; North Carolina National Bank

Robert Rauschenberg
Periwinkle Shaft, 1980
Canvas, current printed images, fabric, mirrors, stuffed fish
Four shaped canvases, each 8′ x 23′; one canvas 14′ x 10′
Foyer of Children's Hospital Medical Center
111 Michigan Avenue, N.W.
Washington, D.C.
Funding: NEA; private donations

George Rickey
Two Open Rectangles Excentric, 1977
Stainless steel
31' x 11' x 6'
Plaza of Prince Jonah Kuhio
Kalanianaole Federal Building and
U.S. Courthouse
300 Ala Moana
Honolulu, Hawaii
Funding: GSA

James Rosati
Heroic Shore Points I, 1977
Painted aluminum
9'9" x 31'10" x 24'
Plaza of Hubert H. Humphrey
Federal Building
330 Independence Avenue
Washington, D.C.
Funding: GSA

Ideogram, 1973
Stainless steel
28' x 23' x 18'
Plaza of World Trade Center
One World Trade Center
New York, New York
Funding: Port Authority of New York
and New Jersey

Tony Rosenthal
Alamo, 1966
Steel
15' x 15' x 15'
Traffic island at Astor Place between
Broadway and 3rd Avenue
New York, New York
Funding: Susan Morris Hilles

Charles Ross
Origin in Colors, 1976
Acrylic, mineral oil
27 prisms, each 9' x 9" x 9"
Lobby of Federal Building
and U.S. Courthouse
100 Centennial Mall North
Lincoln, Nebraska
Funding: GSA

Mark Rothko
Rothko Chapel, 1971
Charcoal, oil on canvas
3 triptychs, each 11' x 15'; 5 panels,
each 11' x 11'
Chapel of Institute of Religion
and Human Development
3900 Yupon Street
Houston, Texas
Funding: The Menil Foundation;
private contributions

Tony Rosenthal
Alamo, 1966
New York, New York

Charles Ross
Origins in Color, 1976
Lincoln, Nebraska

Mark Rothko
Rothko Chapel, 1971
Houston, Texas

George Rickey
Two Open Rectangles Excentric, 1977
Honolulu, Hawaii

George Segal
The Restaurant, 1976
Buffalo, New York

Ned Smyth
Reverent Grove, 1978
St. Thomas, U.S. Virgin Islands

Lucas Samaras
Silent Struggle, 1976
Cor-ten steel, steel
9' x 6' x 1'1"
Plaza of Hale Boggs Federal
Building and U.S. Courthouse
500 Camp Street
New Orleans, Louisiana
Funding: GSA

Charles Searles
Celebration, 1977
Acrylic on canvas
9' x 27'
Cafeteria of William J. Green Jr.
Federal Building
600 Arch Street
Philadelphia, Pennsylvania
Funding: GSA

George Segal
The Restaurant, 1976
Brick, bronze, glass
10' x 16' x 8'
Plaza of Federal Building
111 West Huron Street
Buffalo, New York
Funding: GSA

Richard Serra
St. John's Rotary Arc, 1980
200' x 12' x 2½"
Rotary at Holland Tunnel exit
Hudson, Ericsson, Varick,
and Laight Streets
New York, New York
Funding: Leo Castelli Gallery; Public
Art Fund, Inc.; New York City

Wright's Triangle, 1980
Steel plates
10' x 36' x 36'
Campus of Western Washington
University
Bellingham, Washington
Funding: Allowance from Arntzen Hall
& Environmental Studies Center,
Western Washington University; NEA;
Virginia Wright Fund

Tony Smith
Last, 1979
Orange painted steel
35' x 75'
Plaza of Frank T. Lausche State Office
Building
615 West Superior Avenue
Cleveland, Ohio
Funding: The Cleveland Foundation;
The Ohio Building Authority

Moses, 1968
Steel
46' x 90' x 29'4"
Grounds of Seattle Center
2nd Avenue N.W. and Thomas Street
Seattle, Washington
Funding: City of Seattle; The Virginia
Wright Fund

Ned Smyth
Reverent Grove, 1978
Ceramic and Venetian tile on concrete
10'6" x 8' x 7'
Courtyard of Federal Building
and U.S. Courthouse
Charlotte Amalie, St. Thomas, U.S.
Virgin Islands
Funding: GSA

Michael Steiner
Niagara, 1974
Cor-ten steel
9'3⅜" x 22'2⅓" x 17'10"
Grounds of Wellington
Management Company
Drummers Lane
Valley Forge, Pennsylvania
Funding: Wellington Management
Company

Frank Stella
Joatinga, 1975
Lacquered, etched aluminum
8'6" x 15' x 9"
Lobby of Customhouse
and Federal Building
844 King Street
Wilmington, Delaware
Funding: GSA

Sylvia Stone
Dead Heat, 1979
Brass tubes, plexiglass
8' x 28' x 6'
Facade and plaza of Fort Lauderdale
Federal Building and U.S. Courthouse
299 East Broward Boulevard
Fort Lauderdale, Florida
Funding: GSA

George Sugarman
Greenfield School Wall Complex, 1972
Aluminum
17' x 23' x 18'
Lobby of Albert M. Greenfield School
23rd and Chestnut Streets
Philadelphia, Pennsylvania
Funding: Albert M. Greenfield
Foundation

St. Paul Sculptural Complex, 1971
Painted aluminum
40' x 32' x 29'
Facade of First National Bank
332 Minnesota Avenue
St. Paul, Minnesota
Funding: First National Bank

James Surls
Seaflower, 1978
Steel, wood
24' x 30' x 22'
Plaza of Hastings Keith
Federal Building
53 North 6th Street
New Bedford, Massachusetts
Funding: GSA

William Tarr
Untitled (Dedicated to Dr. Martin Luther King), 1973
Cor-ten steel
28' x 28' x 28'
Grounds of Martin Luther King
High School
Amsterdam Avenue between 65th and
66th Streets
New York, New York
Funding: City of New York

Lenore Tawney
Cloud Series, 1978
Dyed and painted linen threads
16' x 30' x 5'
Lobby of Santa Rosa Federal Building
777 Sonoma Avenue
Santa Rosa, California
Funding: GSA

George Trakas
Untitled, 1979
Concrete, steel, wood
Site dimensions: quadrangle 134' x
90'; ravine contains one path 145'6"
long and one path 119'6" long
Campus of Emery University
Atlanta, Georgia
Funding: Emery University

Ernest Trova
Profile—Canto West, 1975
Stainless steel
22' high
Grounds of Heywood Towers
Apartment House
90th and Amsterdam Avenue
New York, New York
Funding: Kriesler, Borg, Florman
Construction Company

Lenore Tawney
Cloud Series, 1978
Santa Rosa, California

George Trakas
Untitled, 1979
Atlanta, Georgia

David von Schlegell
Untitled, 1972
Boston, Massachusetts

David von Schlegell
Nuevo Mundo, 1977
Stainless steel
18' x 15' x 10'8"
Bicentennial Park
1075 Biscayne Boulevard
Miami, Florida
Funding: City of Miami; NEA

The Gate, 1976
Stainless steel
40' x 37' x 6'
Plaza of Thompson Hill Information
Center
8525 West Skylane Parkway
Duluth, Minnesota
Funding: National Arts Council;
NEA; private donors

Untitled, 1972
Stainless steel
60' x 60' x 16'
India Wharf
85 East India Row
Boston, Massachusetts
Funding: Boston Redevelopment
Authority; Harbor Towers Developers;
I.M. Pei & Partners

Voyage of Ulysses, 1977
Stainless steel, water
16' x 6'6" x 28'4" in 60' diameter pool
Plaza of James A. Byrne Courthouse
and William J. Green, Jr.
Federal Building
6th and Market Streets
Philadelphia, Pennsylvania
Funding: GSA

Peter Voulkos
Barking Sands, 1977
Bronze
6' x 26' x 5'
Plaza of Prince Jonah Kuhio
Kalanianaole Federal Building and
U.S. Courthouse
300 Ala Moana
Honolulu, Hawaii
Funding: GSA

Isaac Witkin
Untitled, 1971
Concrete
18' x 8' x 8'
Vermont Interstate 89 South
Randolph, Vermont
Funding: "Sculpture on the Highway,"
University of Vermont

Jack Youngerman
Rumi's Dance, 1976
Wool
14' x 14'
Lobby of Federal Building
1220 3rd Avenue, S.W.
Portland, Oregon
Funding: GSA

Index of Artworks by Cities

● Books, Reports, and Special Publications

Anderson, Wayne. *American Sculpture in Process: 1930–1970*. New York Graphic Society, Greenwich, Connecticut, 1975.

Barthes, Roland. *The Eiffel Tower and Other Mythologies*. Hill and Wang, New York, 1979.

Cockcroft, Eva, John Weber, and Jim Cockcroft. *Toward a People's Art: The Contemporary Rural Monument*. E.P. Dutton, & Co., New York, 1977.

Collins, DuTot & Associates. *University of Pennsylvania Campus Fine Arts Study*. Collins, DuTot & Associates, Philadelphia, 1970. Mimeographed.

d'Harnoncourt, Anne. *Celebration, Buildings, Art and People*. U.S. General Services Administration, Washington, D.C., 1976.

Franklin Delano Roosevelt Memorial Commission. *The Franklin Delano Roosevelt Memorial*. Report to the President and Congress. Franklin Delano Roosevelt Memorial Commission, May 30, 1978. Mimeographed.

Fried, Frederic, and Edward V. Gilou, Jr. *New York Civic Sculpture*. Dover Publications, New York, 1976.

Goldwater, Robert J. *What is Modern Sculpture?* Museum of Modern Art, New York, 1969.

Goode, James M. *Open-Air Sculpture of Washington: A Comprehensive Historical Guide*. The Smithsonian Institution Press, Washington, D.C., 1974.

Green, Dennis. *% For Art: New Legislation Can Integrate Art and Architecture*. Western States Art Foundation, Inc., Denver, 1976.

Greenberg, David, Kathryn Smith, and Stuart Teacher. *Big Art: Megamurals & Supergraphics*. Running Press, Philadelphia, Pennsylvania, 1977.

Halprin, Lawrence. *Cities*. Reinhold Publishing Corporation, New York, 1972.

Halprin, Lawrence and Associates. *Environmental Criteria for the California State Capitol Plan*. California Department of General Services, Sacramento, 1968.

Institute of Contemporary Art, University of Pennsylvania. *Urban Encounters: A Map of Public Art in Philadelphia*. Institute of Contemporary Art, University of Pennsylvania, Philadelphia, 1980.

Kassler, Elizabeth B. *Modern Gardens and the Landscape*. Museum of Modern Art, New York, 1964.

Krauss, Rosalind E. *Passages in Modern Sculpture*. Viking Press, New York, 1977.

Krier, Rob. *Urban Space*. Rizzoli International Publications, Inc., New York, 1979.

Lederer, Joseph, and Arley Bondarin. *All Around The Town: Walking Guide to Outdoor Sculpture in New York City*. Charles Scribner's Sons, New York, 1975.

Lynch, Kevin. *The Image of the City*. The M.I.T. Press, Cambridge, Massachusetts, and London, 1979.

Maldonado, Tomás. *Design, Nature and Revolution: Toward A Critical Ecology*. Harper and Row, New York, 1972.

McKinzie, Richard D. *The New Deal for Artists*. Princeton University Press, Princeton, 1973.

Mecklenburg, Virginia. *The Public As Patron, A History of the Treasury Department Mural Program Illustrated with Paintings from the Collection of the University of Maryland Art Gallery*. University of Maryland, College Park, Maryland, 1979.

Miles, Don C., Robert S. Cook, and Cameron B. Roberts. *Plazas for People*. New York City Department of City Planning, New York, 1978.

Murphy, Levy, Wurman. *Penn's Landing: Philadelphia's Urban Waterfront*. Old Philadelphia Development Corporation, Penn's Landing Corporation, Philadelphia, 1975.

O'Connor, Francis V., ed. *Art for the Millions, Essays from the 1930's by Artists and Administrators of the WPA Federal Art Project*. New York Graphic Society, Greenwich, Connecticut, 1973.

O'Connor, Francis V., ed. *Federal Support for the Visual Arts: The New Deal and Now*. New York Graphic Society, Greenwich, Connecticut, 1969, 2nd edition, 1971.

O'Connor, Francis V., ed. *The New Deal Art Projects, An Anthology of Memoirs*. The Smithsonian Institution Press, Washington, D.C., 1972.

Park, Marlene, and Gerald E. Markowitz. *New Deal for Art, The Government Art Projects of the 1930's with Examples from New York City and State*. The Gallery Association of New York State, Inc., New York, 1977.

Perlman, Bernard B. *1% Art in Civic Architecture*. RTKL Associates, Inc., Baltimore, 1973.

Redevelopment Authority, City of Philadelphia. *Annual Report, 1975*. Redevelopment Authority, City of Philadelphia, Philadelphia, 1975.

Redevelopment Authority, City of Philadelphia. *City Art*. The Fine Arts Program of the Redevelopment Authority, City of Philadelphia, Philadelphia, 1979.

Redstone, Louis G. *Art in Architecture*. McGraw-Hill Company, Inc., New York, 1968.

Robinette, Margaret. *Outdoor Sculpture: Object and Environment*. Whitney Library of Design, an imprint of Watson-Guptill Publications, New York, 1976.

Rockefeller Center, Inc. *The Art Program of Rockefeller Center and Its Contributing Artists*. Rockefeller Center, Inc., New York, 1972.

Special Commission on Art in State Buildings. *A Program to Integrate Art and State Buildings*. Report of the Special Commission on Art in State Buildings to Governor William G. Miliken. Lansing, Michigan, January, 1978. Mimeographed.

Sandler, Irving. *A Report on Public Art to the Chairman of the National Endowment for the Arts*. Washington, D.C., 1973. Mimeographed.

Scully, Vincent. *The Earth, The Temple and The Gods*. Yale University Press, New Haven, Connecticut, 1962.

Sky, Allison, ed. *On Site V.P. (Visual Pollution)*. Site, Inc., New York, 1971.

Solomon, Jay. *Art in Architecture Program*. U.S. General Services Administration, Washington, D.C., 1977.

Stearns-Phillips, Daydre. *Western's Outdoor Museum*. Western Washington University, Bellingham, Washington, 1979.

Thalacker, Donald W. *The Place of Art in the World of Architecture*. Chelsea House Publishers, New York, 1980.

U.S. Department of Transportation. *Design, Art, and Architecture in Transportation*. Report to the Secretary of Transportation. U.S. Government Printing Office, Washington, D.C., Annually, 1977–1980.

U.S. General Services Administration. *Art in Architecture Program*. U.S. General Services Administration, Washington, D.C., 1979.

Wainwright, Nicholas B., ed. *Sculpture of a City: Philadelphia's Treasures in Bronze and Stone*. Walker Publishing Company, Inc., New York, 1974.

Zucker, Paul. *Town and Square: From Agora to the Village Green*. Columbia University Press, New York, and London, 1959.

● Periodicals

Alloway, Lawrence. "Monumental Art at Cincinnati," *Arts Magazine*, November 1970, pp. 32–36.

Alloway, Lawrence. "One Sculpture," *Arts Magazine*, May 1971, pp. 22–24.

Alloway, Lawrence. "Public Sculpture for the Post-Heroic Age," *Art in America*, October 1979, pp. 9–11.

Alloway, Lawrence. "The Public Sculpture Problem," *Studio International*, October 1972, pp. 122–125.

Ashton, Dore. "Unconventional Techniques in Sculpture," *Studio International*, January 1965, pp. 22–25.

Baker, A.T. "Shaping Water into Art," *Time Magazine*, September 12, 1977, pp. 32–33.

Baker, Elizabeth C. "Mark di Suvero's Burgundian Season," *Art in America*, May-June 1974, pp. 59–63.

Bongartz, Roy. "Where the Monumental Sculptors Go," *Art News*, February 1976, pp. 34–37.

Carpenter, Edward K. "Urban Art," *Design and Environment*, Summer 1974, pp. 17–27.

Carter, Malcolm N. "The F.D.R. Memorial," *Art News*, October 1978, pp. 50–57.

Celant, Germano. "Artspaces," *Studio International*, September-October 1975, pp. 114–123.

Davis, Douglas. "Public Art: The Taming of the Vision," *Art in America*, May-June 1974, pp. 84–85.

Dean, Andrea O. "Art in the Environment," *AIA Journal*, October 1976, p. 33.

Dean, Andrea O. "Bunshaft and Noguchi: An Uneasy but Highly Productive Architect-Artist Collaboration," *AIA Journal*, October 1976, pp. 52–55.

Dean, Andrea O. "Grand Rapids Becomes a Showplace of the Use of Sculpture in Public Spaces," *AIA Journal*, October 1976, pp. 40–43.

Filler, Martin. "The Magic Fountain," *Progressive Architecture*, November 1978, pp. 86–87.

Foote, Nancy. "Monument-Sculpture-Earthwork," *Artforum*, October 1979, pp. 32–37.

Forgey, Benjamin. "A New Vision: Public Places with Sculpture," *Smithsonian*, October 1975, pp. 51–57.

Forgey, Benjamin. "It Takes More than an Outdoor Site to Make Sculpture Public," *Art News*, September 1980, pp. 84–89.

60

Freedman, Doris. "Public Sculpture," *Design and Environment*, Summer 1974, p. 19.

Franz, Gina. "How Public Is Public Sculpture?" *The New Art Examiner*, February 1980, Section 2, p. 3.

Gilbert-Rolfe, Jeremy. "Capital Follies," *Artforum*, September 1978, pp. 66–67.

Glueck, Grace. "New Sculpture under the Sun, from Staten Island to the Bronx," *The New York Times*, August 3, 1979, Section C, pp. 1, 15.

Gortazar, Fernando Gonzalez. "Sculptures as 'Vitalizing Elements' in Superficial Urban Settings," *Landscape Architecture*, November 1976, pp. 534–536.

Goldin, Amy. "The Esthetic Ghetto: Some Thoughts about Public Art," *Art in America*, May-June 1974, pp. 30–35.

Greenberg, Clement. "The New Sculpture," *Partisan Review*, June 1949, pp. 637–642.

Harney, Andy Leon. "The Proliferating One Percent Programs for the Use of Art in Public Buildings," *AIA Journal*, October 1976, pp. 35–39.

Hitchcock, Henry-Russell, and William Seale. "How Nebraska Acquired a State Capitol Like No Other," *AIA Journal*, October 1976, pp. 56–61.

Huxtable, Ada Louise. "Public Sculpture-A City's Most Pervasive Art," *The New York Times*, September 15, 1974, Section D, p. 29.

Kepes, Gyorgy. "The Artist as Environmentalist: A Proposal," *Ekistics*, November 1972, pp. 372–374.

Kramer, Hilton. "Sculpture is Having and Coming-Out," *The New York Times*, February 19, 1978, Section D , p. 29.

Kramer, Hilton. "Sculpture on the Streets," *The New York Times*, July 15, 1979, Section D, p. 25.

Krauss, Rosalind. "Sculpture in the Expanded Field," *October, No. 8*, Spring 1979, pp. 31–44.

Lacy, Bill N. "New Guidelines for Federal Architecture," *Art in America*, September-October 1972, p. 19.

Lippard, Lucy R. "Complexes: Architectural Sculpture in Nature," *Art in America*, January-February 1979, pp. 86–97.

Marlin, William. "Sprucing up a City," *Saturday Review*, February 7, 1976, pp. 50–52.

Meadmore, Clement, Edward Fry, and Barbara Rose. "Symposium on Three Dimensions," *Arts Magazine*, January 1975, pp. 62–65.

Noah, Barbara. "Cost-Effective Earth Art," *Art in America*, January 1980, pp. 12–15.

Nochlin, Linda. "The Paterson Strike Pageant of 1913," *Art in America*, May-June 1974, pp. 64–68.

Nochlin, Linda. "The Realist Criminal and The Abstract Law," *Art in America*, September-October 1973, pp. 54–61.

O'Doherty, Brian. "The Grand Rapids Challenge," *Art in America*, January-February 1974, pp. 78–79.

O'Doherty, Brian. "Public Art and the Government: A Progress Report," *Art in America*, May-June 1974, pp. 44–49.

O'Doherty, Brian. "Inside the White Cube: Notes on the Gallery Space, Part I," *Artforum*, March 1976, pp. 24–32; ". . . :The Eye and the Spectator, Part II," April 1976, pp. 26–34; ". . . : Context as Content, Part III," November 1976, pp. 38–44.

Peterson, Iver. "In a Mellower Detroit, River Park Revives," *The New York Times*, June 17, 1979, p. 22.

Radoczy, Albert. "On Correlating Sculpture with Architecture," *Arts and Architecture*, April 1948, pp. 28–30.

Robbins, Corinne. "New York: 'Public Sculpture in Public Places'," *Arts Magazine*, Summer 1967, pp. 50–51.

Rose, Barbara. "Looking at American Sculpture," *Artforum*, February 1965, pp. 29–36.

Rose, Barbara. "Public Art's Big Hit," *Vogue*, July 1977, pp. 118, 145.

Rose, Barbara. "Shall We Have a Renaissance?" *Art in America*, March-April 1967, pp. 30–39.

Scott, Nancy. "Politics on a Pedestal," *Art Journal*, Spring 1979, pp. 190–196.

Senie, Harriet. "Urban Sculpture: Cultural Tokens or Ornaments to Life?" *Art News*, September 1979, pp. 108–114.

Shapiro, David. "Sculpture as Experience: The Monument that Suffered," *Art in America*, May-June 1974, pp. 55–58.

Sinclair, Stephen. "When Art Meets the Community," *NEA Cultural Post*, March-April 1980, p. 1, 8–9.

Slavin, Maeve. "Art and Architecture, Can They Ever Meet Again?" *Interiors*, March 1980, pp. 78–81, 102.

Sommer, Robert. "People's Art," *AIA Journal*, December 1972, pp. 29–34.

Sonfist, Alan. "Natural Phenomena as Public Monuments," *Tracks 3*, 1–2, Spring 1977, pp. 44–47.

Stevens, Mark, Mary Hager, and Maggie Malone. "Sculpture out in the Open," *Newsweek*, August 18, 1980, pp. 70–71.

Tacha, Athena. "Rhythm as Form," *Landscape Architecture*, May 1978, pp. 196–205.

Tarzan, Dolores. "Art, The Public, and Public Art," *Seattle Times*, September 21, 1980, Section F, pp. 1, 6.

Tarzan, Dolores. "The Best and the Worst in Public Art," *Seattle Times*, September 21, 1980, Section F, p. 1.

Tarzan, Dolores. "The Earthwork," *Seattle Times*, September 23, 1980, Section E, p. 1.

Tarzan, Dolores. "Hot Debate over Expenditure for Art in King County Cooler," *Seattle Times*, September 22, 1980, Section E, p. 4.

Tighe, Mary Ann. "Di Suvero in Grand Rapids: The Public Prevails," *Art in America*, March-April 1977, pp. 12–15.

Trachtenberg, Marvin. "The Statue of Liberty: Transparent Banality or Avant-Garde Conundrum?" *Art in America*, May-June 1974, pp. 36–43.

Tuchman, Phyllis. "Sculptors Mass in Toronto," *Art in America*, September-October 1978, pp. 15–16, 21–23.

Vrchota, Janet. "Grand Rapids Case Study," *Design and Environment*, Summer 1974, pp. 28–31.

Vrchota, Joliene. "Urban Art Portfolio," *Design and Environment*, Summer 1974, pp. 32–35.

●Exhibition Catalogues

Across the Nation: Fine Art for Federal Buildings, 1972-1979. Essay by Joshua C. Taylor. National Collection of Fine Arts, The Smithsonian Institution, Washington, D.C., 1980.

American Sculpture of the Sixties. Essays by Dore Ashton and Lucy R. Lippard, edited by Maurice Tuchman. Los Angeles Museum of Art, Los Angeles, 1967.

Art in Public Places and Contemporary Sculpture in a Rural Community. State College Office of the Arts, Big Rapids, Michigan, 1979.

Artpark: The Program in Visual Arts. Artpark, Lewiston, New York, 1974, 1976, 1977.

Earthworks: Land Reclamation as Sculpture. King County Arts Commision, and the King County Department of Public Works, King County, Washington, 1979.

14 Sculptors: The Industrial Edge. Essays by Christopher Finch, Martin Friedman, and Barbara Rose. Walker Art Center, Minneapolis, 1969.

Grand Rapids Project/Robert Morris. Introduction by Edward F. Fry, essay by Connie Oosting. Grand Rapids Art Museum, Grand Rapids, 1975.

Isamu Noguchi: The Sculpture of Spaces. Whitney Museum of American Art, New York, 1980. Statement by the artist.

Monumenta. Introduction by Sam Hunter, essay by Hugh M. Davies and Sally E. Yard. Monumenta Newport, Inc., Newport, Rhode Island, 1974.

Monumental Art. Essays by Lawrence Alloway, Van Meter Ames, John Hightower, William A. Leonard, and Douglas McAgy. Contemporary Arts Museum, Cinncinati, 1970.

New Urban Monuments. Essay by Robert Doty. Akron Art Institute, Akron, 1977.

9 Artists/9 Spaces. Essay by Richard Koshalek, Minnesota State Arts Council, Minneapolis, 1970.

Noguchi's Imaginary Landscapes. Essay by Martin Friedman. Walker Art Center, Minneapolis, 1978.

Object into Monument, Claes Oldenburg. Essay by Barbara Haskell. Pasadena Art Museum, Pasadena, 1971.

The Public Monument and Its Audience. Essays by Marianne Doezema and June Hargrove. Cleveland Museum of Art, Cleveland, 1977.

Public Sculpture/Urban Environment. Introduction by George Neubert. Oakland Museum, Oakland, California, 1974.

Quintessence. Introduction by Paul R. Wick. City Beautiful Council of Dayton, Ohio and Wright State University Department of Art, Dayton. Fall 1977, Fall 1978.

Robert Morris/Projects. Introduction by Edward F. Fry. Institute of Contemporary Art, University of Pennsylvania, Philadelphia, 1974.

S/10 Sculpture Today. Introduction by David P. Silcox, Chairman. Published in cooperation with the International Sculpture Center, Princeton, 1978.

Sculpture off the Pedestal. Essay by Barbara Rose. Grand Rapids Art Museum, Grand Rapids, 1973.

● Seminars and Conferences

Art and Mass Public and the Underground: A Toronto Venture. Paper by Theodore Allen Heinrich delivered at the third working session of the annual meeting of the International Council of Museums, The National Gallery of Norway, Oslo, Norway, 1978. Mimeographed.

Art in Public Places. Symposium organized by Washington State University, Seattle, Washington, October 1978. Seattle Arts Commission.

The Arts and City Planning . . . Making Cities Livable. Conference organized by the American Council for the Arts, San Antonio, Texas, December 11-13, 1979.

Arts Renewal: Boston's Visual Environment 1974-1984. Symposium organized by the Institute of Contemporary Art, Boston, Massachusetts, in cooperation with the Mayor's Office of Cultural Affairs, The Boston Visual Artists Union, and the New England School of Design, May 1-4, 1974.

California International Sculpture Symposium. Symposium organized by Department of Art, California State University at Long Beach, Long Beach, California, 1965.

International Sculpture Conference. Organized by the International Sculpture Center, Princeton, New Jersey. Washington, D.C., June 4-6, 1980.

Monumental Art in Our Society. Public Art and Public Policies. Symposium organized by the Contemporary Arts Museum, Cincinnati, Ohio, July 1980. Conference text prepared by Jayne Merkle, *Public Art: Do We Need It?* Mimeographed.

On Human Dimensions. John E. Walley Commemoration Design Conference, University of Illinois, May 20, 1975. Papers presented by Benny Andrews, Margaret Burroughs, Joseph Carreiro, Barry Commoner, Edgar Kaufmann, Jr., Ian McHarg, Brian O'Doherty, Studs Terkel, and William H. Whyte. University of Illinois, Chicago, Illinois, 1976.

Open Plan 79, the American Monument. Series of seminars and lectures sponsored by the Institute for Architecture and Urban Studies, New York, New York, September through December, 1979.

Vermont International Sculpture Symposium. University of Vermont Department of Art, Burlington, Vermont, 1973. Conference brochure with essay by Lois Ingram, published by George Little Press, Inc., Burlington, Vermont, 1973.

Lenders to the Exhibition

Stephen Antonakos

City of Baltimore, Department of
Housing and Community
Development

Jennifer Bartlett

Richard Bellamy

Charles Cowles

Mark di Suvero

Rafael Ferrer

Richard Fleischner

Red Grooms

Lawrence Halprin
Lawrence Halprin and Associates

Hamilton Gallery of Contemporary
Art

Lloyd Hamrol

Robert Irwin

J. Roberts Jennings

Mr. and Mrs. M.S. Keeler II

King County Arts
Commission, Seattle

Nicole Levin

Joel Meyerowitz

Robert Miller Gallery

Milwaukee Exposition
Convention Center Arena

Charles Moore
Urban Innovations Group

National Endowment
for the Arts
Washington, D.C.

Isamu Noguchi

Noguchi Fountains Inc.

Claes Oldenburg

The Pace Gallery

George Sugarman

Athena Tacha

Witkin Gallery

ICA Advisory Board

ICA Staff

Photo Credits

64

Charles Adler (Heizer), p. 12

Jeremiah O. Bragstad (Halprin), pp. 24, 25

Colleen Chartier (Morris), p. 28

Mark Cohn (Venturi, Rauch, and Scott Brown), p. 30

Tom Crane (Nevelson), pp. 19, 51

Maude Dorr (Halprin), pp. 22, 23, 32

Gene Dwiggins (Fleischner), p. 48

eeva-inkeri (Bartlett), p. 40

Glen Fleck (Halprin), p. 24

Olivia Georgia (Antonakos), p. 37

John Gotman (Ferrer), p. 44

Greg Heins (Irwin), p. 50

Balthazar Korab (Calder), p. 10 (Noguchi), pp. 30, 31, (Saarinen), cover, p. 9

Arthur Lavine (Dubuffet), p. 16

Fred Lyons (Halprin), p. 23

Norman McGrath (Moore), pp. 33, 45

Gaye Meekins (di Suvero), p. 12

Eugene Mopsik (Installation at Institute of Contemporary Art), pp. 35, 36, 38, 42

Hans Namuth (Rosenthal), p. 53

Alan Ostrom (Grooms), p. 32

The Pace Gallery (von Schlegell), p. 56

Redevelopment Authority of Philadelphia (Oldenburg), p. 17

Craig VanderLende (Calder), p. 10

Typeset and printed in an edition of 2000 on Cameo dull 100 lb. cover and text by The Falcon Press, Philadelphia

Design/Jerome Cloud
Production Assistance/Penelope Malish